ISBN 978-0-282-52076-2
PIBN 10854737

PEABODY MUSEUM

OF

AMERICAN ARCHAEOLOGY AND ETHNOLOGY

HARVARD UNIVERSITY

MEMOIRS

VOLUME II

CAMBRIDGE, MASS.
PUBLISHED BY THE MUSEUM
1901–1903

University Press:
John Wilson and Son, Cambridge, U.S.A.

MEMOIRS

OF THE

PEABODY MUSEUM OF AMERICAN ARCHAEOLOGY AND ETHNOLOGY, HARVARD UNIVERSITY

VOL. II—No. 1

RESEARCHES IN THE CENTRAL PORTION OF THE USUMATSINTLA VALLEY

REPORT OF EXPLORATIONS FOR THE MUSEUM, 1898–1900

BY

TEOBERT MALER

CAMBRIDGE:

PUBLISHED BY THE MUSEUM

1901

PUBLICATIONS

OF THE

Peabody Museum of American Archaeology and Ethnology.

Annual Reports. 8vo.

VOLUME I contains the first nine Reports (1868–1876) with index. 309 pages. Price, bound in cloth, $5.00.

VOLUME II contains the 10th, 11th, 12th, and 13th Reports (1877–1880), with many illustrations and index. 782 pages. Price, bound in cloth, $6.00.

VOLUME III contains the 14th, 15th, 16th, 17th, 18th, 19th, and 20th Reports (1881–1887). 586 pages, with illustrations and index. Price, bound in cloth, $3.00.

VOLUME IV contains the 21st, 22d, 23d, and 24th Reports (1887–1890). Price, in paper, $1.00.

The 25th and following Reports are printed in the Annual Reports of the President of Harvard University.

Archaeological and Ethnological Papers. 8vo.

VOLUME I — **Number 1.** STANDARD OR HEAD-DRESS? — An historical essay on a relic of Ancient Mexico. By ZELIA NUTTALL. 52 pages and 3 colored plates. 1888. $1.00.

Number 2. The KARANKAWA INDIANS, THE COAST PEOPLE OF TEXAS. — By ALBERT S. GATSCHET, with notes by C. A. HAMMOND and ALICE W. OLIVER, and a vocabulary obtained from Alice W. Oliver. 104 pages with map. 1891. $1.00.

Number 3. THE ATLATL OR SPEAR-THROWER OF THE ANCIENT MEXICANS. — By ZELIA NUTTALL. 36 pages and 3 plates. 1891. 50 cents.

Number 4. REPORT UPON PILE-STRUCTURES IN NAAMAN'S CREEK, NEAR CLAYMONT, DELAWARE. — By HILBORNE T. CRESSON. 24 pages and Illustrations. 1892. 30 cents.

Number 5. A STUDY OF OMAHA INDIAN MUSIC; INCLUDING TRANSCRIPTIONS OF 92 SONGS, WORDS AND MUSIC. — By ALICE C. FLETCHER, aided by FRANCIS LA FLESCHE. With a Report on the Structural Peculiarities of the Music, by JOHN COMFORT FILLMORE. 152 pages. 1893. $1.25.

Number 6. PREHISTORIC BURIAL PLACES IN MAINE. — By C. C. WILLOUGHBY. 52 pages, 4 plates, 50 illustrations in text. 1898. $1.00.

Number 7. (Completing the volume, not yet printed.)

VOLUME II — THE FUNDAMENTAL PRINCIPLES OF OLD AND NEW WORLD CIVILIZATION. — By ZELIA NUTTALL. 602 pages, 7 plates, 73 illustrations in text, and Index. 1901. $3.00 in paper. $3.50 in cloth.

Memoirs of the Museum. 4to.

VOLUME I — **Number 1.** PREHISTORIC RUINS OF COPAN, HONDURAS. — A Preliminary Report of the Explorations by the Museum, 1891–95. 48 pages. Large map, illustrations in text, and 8 plates. 1896. $1.50.

Number 2. EXPLORATIONS OF THE CAVE OF LOLTUN, YUCATAN. — By E. H. THOMPSON. 22 pages. Illustrations in text, and 8 plates. 1897. $1.00.

Number 3. The CHULTUNES OF LABNÁ. — By E. H. THOMPSON. 20 pages. Illustrations in text, and 13 plates. 1897. $1.25.

Number 4. RESEARCHES IN THE ULOA VALLEY. — By GEORGE BYRON GORDON. 44 pages. Illustrations in text, map, and 12 plates. 1898.

Number 5. CAVERNS OF COPAN. — By GEORGE BYRON GORDON. 12 pages, map, and 1 plate. 1898. Nos. 4 and 5 under one cover, $1.50.

(This volume not yet completed.)

VOLUME II — **Number 1.** RESEARCHES IN THE CENTRAL PORTION OF THE USUMATSINTLA VALLEY. By TEOBERT MALER. 75 pages, 33 plates, 26 illustrations in text. 1901. $3.50.

Regular subscribers will receive the publications as issued, at 20 per cent less than specified price.

See page 3 of Cover.

Address: PEABODY MUSEUM, Cambridge, Mass.

Agents for the Museum Publications,

Bernard Quaritch, 15 Piccadilly, London. Karl W. Hiersemann, Koenigsstrasse 3, Leipsig.

CONTENTS.

For Contents of this volume, see pages 3 and 79.
For Lists of Plates, see pages 5 and 81.

ILLUSTRATIONS IN THE TEXT.

MEMOIRS

OF THE

PEABODY MUSEUM OF AMERICAN ARCHAEOLOGY AND
ETHNOLOGY, HARVARD UNIVERSITY

Vol. II—No. 1

RESEARCHES IN THE CENTRAL PORTION

OF THE

USUMATSINTLA VALLEY

Report of Explorations for the Museum, 1898–1900

BY

TEOBERT MALER

CAMBRIDGE:
PUBLISHED BY THE MUSEUM
1901

UNIVERSITY PRESS:
JOHN WILSON AND SON, CAMBRIDGE, U.S.A.

BargainBookStores.com

Name: David A Pritzke
Email: daplibro@aol.com
Order Date: 7/19/2018 8:05:51 PM
Ship Method: Standard

Order #: 00595052AB
PO #: PO-18023011-IBC
Seller Order: 147176914

Qty	ISBN/UPC	Title	Price
1		Memoirs of the Peabody Museum of American Archaeology and Ethnology, Harvard University, Vol. 2: No. 1, Researches in the Central Portion of the Usuma (Paperback or Softback)	$14.47

Questions:

Subtotal:	$14.47
Shipping:	$0.00
Tax:	$0.00
Total:	$14.47

S | 1

00595052AB

TO REORDER YOUR UPS DIRECT THERMAL LABELS:

1. Access our supply ordering website at **UPS.COM**®
   or contact UPS at 800-877-8652

2. Please refer to Label # 01774006 when ordering.

Shipper agrees to the UPS Terms and Conditions of Carriage/Service found at www.ups.com and at UPS service centers. If carriage includes an ultimate destination or stop in a country other than the country of departure, the Convention on the Unification of Certain Rules Relating to International Transportation By Air as amended (Warsaw Convention) or the Montreal Convention may apply and in most cases limits UPS's liability for loss or damage to cargo. Shipments transported partly or solely by road into or from a country that is party to the Convention on the Contract for the International Carriage of Goods By Road (CMR) are subject to the provisions in the CMR notwithstanding any clause to the contrary in the UPS Terms. Except as otherwise governed by such international conventions or other mandatory law, the UPS terms limit UPS's liability for damage, loss or delay of this shipment. There are no stopping places which are agreed upon at the time of tender of the shipment and UPS reserves the right to route the shipment in any way it deems appropriate.

01774006 RRD

CONTENTS.

LIST OF PLATES.

EDITORIAL NOTE.

THIS report by Mr. Teobert Maler covers his explorations of several groups of ancient ruins in the valley of the Usumatsintla and his visit to the Lacantuns of Lake Pethá. It is the first of a series which will make known the results of the researches which Mr. Maler is conducting under the auspices of the Museum.

In his graphic and entertaining style, Mr. Maler gives us vivid pictures of the wild beauty and tropical luxuriousness of the country through which he journeys; and in the relation of his dealings with the Lacantuns he gives us glimpses of the life and customs of these little-known denizens of the jungle about Lake Pethá.

Mr. Maler has spent many years in Mexico and Central America, and has examined and photographed many of the prehistoric ruins and sculptures of that region. The beautiful photographs which he has so skilfully taken — notwithstanding the difficulties to be overcome — have made his name familiar to all students of American archaeology; and it will be gratifying to all Americanists to read this account of Mr. Maler's explorations and to examine the interesting series of photographs here published.

Mr. Maler's map of the Central Usumatsintla Valley and his plan of the ruins of Piedras Negras, here reproduced, will awaken a new interest in the great cities of the past, which are still hidden in the jungles of Central America.

This report was written in German by Mr. Maler, and has been translated into English by Miss Selma Wesselhoeft, assisted by Miss A. M. Parker. Every effort has been made to secure an accurate translation and to keep the decisive style of the author; while the Editor has respected the fact that the author could not revise the proofs. Mr. Maler is therefore responsible for the opinions expressed and the statements made, as well as for the spelling of proper names, in which he sometimes differs from the generally accepted orthography.

The reproduction of the photographs has been admirably accomplished by the heliotype process, special care having been taken by the Heliotype

Company to accurately reproduce the original prints. This part of the work has been carefully supervised by Mr. C. C. Willoughby.

It is a pleasure to acknowledge, in behalf of the Museum, our indebtedness to Mr. Charles P. Bowditch of the Museum Faculty for his continued interest and co-operation in the work pertaining to Central America. Our thanks are also tendered to all the subscribers whose generous aid has made it possible to continue our researches in Central America and to publish the results.

F. W. PUTNAM,
Curator of the Museum.

HARVARD UNIVERSITY, CAMBRIDGE,
October, 1901.

SUBSCRIBERS

TO THE FUND FOR THE ENCOURAGEMENT OF CENTRAL AMERICAN RESEARCH.

STEPHEN SALISBURY, Worcester
CHARLES P. BOWDITCH, Boston
AUGUSTUS HEMENWAY, Boston
JUDGE FRANCIS C. LOWELL, Boston
MR. & MRS. HENRY PICKERING, Boston
MISS ELLEN F. MASON, Boston
EDWARD S. GREW, Boston
MRS. G. G. LOWELL, Boston
GEORGE A. NICKERSON, Boston
NATHANIEL THAYER, Boston
ELIOT C. LEE, Boston
MISS MARY L. WARE, Boston
MISS CAROLINE P. STOKES, New York

RESEARCHES IN THE USUMATSINTLA VALLEY.

I.

LA REFORMA.

IN the middle of January, 1898, after I had engaged four men in Tenosique and had finished other preparations for my journey, I left this starting-point of my expeditions, intending to explore the route from Chinikihá to Xupá, and to go to Palenque if circumstances allowed, and then to push on to the great Lake of Pethá and the settlements of the Lacantuns.

Accompanied by two of my men and our luggage, I travelled in a cayuco up to Pomoná, a small settlement two leagues above Tenosique (see map, Plate I), while the other two men brought the pack animals by land to the crossing-place at Pomoná, where they safely crossed the Usumatsintla, with the help of the cayucos and the men which I sent to their assistance after my arrival. Pomoná comprises only a few huts, inhabited by people belonging to the sugar rancho of San Antonio on the opposite shore.

We spent the night at Pomoná; on the next day we took the road through the forests to La Reforma, where we arrived after a two days' journey. La Reforma is a large settlement belonging to the firm of Romano, and lies close to the right shore of the Chacamax, perhaps ten leagues from Pomoná and Tenosique.

Not being acquainted with the managers who were in charge of this montería, I naturally had some difficulty in making them understand the object of my coming, and in obtaining their permission to unload my luggage and to shelter my men in some corner of one of their buildings. By degrees, however, friendly relations were established with these gentlemen. Gradually they began to take an interest in my not uninteresting expeditions, and also to render me some assistance. One of the managers was a Spaniard, Isidoro Mucha by name; the other was an engineer, Felippe Molina, from the city of Mexico. Both were agreeable and cultivated men.

A road — which is in a frightful condition during the greater part of the year — leads from La Reforma to the distant settlement, on the Lacantun River, belonging to the same firm of Romano, and called *Los Tzendales*. This forest road runs directly through the vast wilderness in which the scattered remnants of the Maya-Lacantuns live.

Southward from the cluster of buildings of La Reforma, a small mountain range is visible, the crest of which forms an extensive plateau, on which the ruins of a little ancient city lie hidden among the high forest trees. Although the monteros had found nothing of importance there, as the ruins lay within easy reach I deemed it advisable to explore them. Following the road to Tzendales for two kilometres, and then turning to the right where the road is crossed by a small stream and a giant ceiba lifts its top to the sky, we entered the forest. Ascending the slopes, we soon reached the ruins, which were quite numerous and often quite imposing, — foundation walls, levelled areas, heaps of ruins, etc. Finally, we also discovered the principal temple, which crowned the platform of a massive, well-preserved substructure about six metres in height. It was still possible to determine the position of the various apartments of this edifice. I thoroughly explored these ruins and their neighborhood for sculptured stones, but in vain. All I found was a large, thick stone slab (sacrificial table ?) on which, however, there was no drawing of any kind.

I called these ruins "Las Ruinas de La Reforma."

II.

CHINIKIHÁ.

THE name Chinikihá (Tšinikihá), or Chinikilhá, admits of a twofold interpretation : chi-nīkil-há (tši-nīkil-há) = "mouth or opening of the disappearing water," in allusion to the river passing through a rocky tunnel not far from the ruins. Or it may also be that there is in this region a tree named chinikil (nic, nicté, in names of plants always signify "flower"). Hence the name — without putting too much emphasis on the second *i* — can also signify "water where the chinikil tree grows."

I had long known that there was a large ruined city on the Chinikihá River, but it was not until the middle of January, 1898, after making my headquarters in La Reforma, that I was able to undertake the thorough exploration of these ruins. To reach them we first took the *camino de Tzendales*, and after travelling for about two leagues (or for two hours), we turned off to the left, following the path of an abandoned montería, El Clavo, and by turning still farther to the left, we soon crossed the Chinikihá and reached the *camino viejo de Tenosique*, a road which passes straight through the ruined city. Here on this path, which is now seldom used, we built a small palm-leaf hut, *champa*, at a spot convenient for bathing in the river and for providing ourselves with water.

We first explored all the remains on the right of the road, but found nothing but remnants of walls and terraces, with the exception that in one building we found small rear rooms in a half-preserved condition; everything else was completely in ruins. Then we followed the road to Tenosique for nearly two kilometres, to the end of the mountain pass, where the path running between high cliffs begins to descend into the valley of the Usumatsintla. Though it was a difficult task, we climbed these cliffs and enjoyed a magnificent view of the endless, wooded lowlands through which the Usumatsintla rolls. From these lofty heights our view extended as far as Balancan and beyond. But finding no structures on these cliffs, we returned wearied to our camp.

On the following day we undertook the exploration of that portion of the town which lies on the left of the road. Here we found the main mass of the buildings, which, it is true, are mostly in ruins. Two groups of buildings of noble proportions especially attracted our attention. In one the outlines of a large court were recognizable, intersected by a high and massive structure. The rooms which formerly bordered this court were in ruins, but from out the débris projected great lintels. These I examined in the hope of finding sculptures on the under side, but, alas, in vain!

The other larger group of buildings, which in past years had more particularly fallen a prey to the depredations of the woodcutters exploiting these woods, was especially difficult to rediscover, since, when the woodcutters abandoned this region, the forest had been set on fire and everything was now concealed by the dense vegetation.

Mr. Molina himself came to our assistance from La Reforma, bringing with him some of the most experienced of the elder monteros. And it was only with this help that we were successful in finding the ruins.

A great pyramid, rising in several terraces, once formed the substructure of the principal temple, which now like the adjacent apartments has fallen to ruin. From among the débris the woodcutters — who, I regret to say, seem to busy themselves, incidentally and in a manner quite uncalled for, with archaeology, but naturally only after the style of woodcutters — had taken out a slab bearing inscriptions, intending to carry it away with them, but finding it too heavy, they left it lying on the side of the pyramid and contented themselves with knocking off a corner to take with them as a "specimen"!

I succeeded in finding this slab, and at once perceived that it was part of a stone table, which had rested against a wall, and whose three exposed (naturally narrow) faces were ornamented with very delicately executed hieroglyphs in bas-relief, while the top (at least of the portion which I found) also had an inscription, which, however, was incised.

Here was another instance of the mischief arising from the meddling of ignorant people. If the men had simply left the slab on the spot where they found it, it would have been an easy matter for me to have dug a little further and the missing portion would undoubtedly have come to light. Now, of course, no one can surmise in what part of the huge pyramid of ruins, overgrown with trees, this table stood. We must perforce be content, therefore, with the mutilated fragment here discovered.

The table is chiselled out of the finest limestone. Its breadth is sixty-two centimetres, the length of the part found is seventy-five, the width of the band of glyphs is seven, but the general thickness of the stone is somewhat more. The incised inscription of the top formerly consisted (according to my calculation) of twenty-four squares containing glyphs in two rows of twelve each. Of the first row eight are preserved, and of the second six. The missing squares belong to the broken-off corner. The first seven glyph-squares of the outer band were preserved; then, on the same side, there were probably four more, and around the broken-off corner, on the long side, probably six more; then followed seven well-preserved squares to the edge where the missing portion of the table formerly joined.

I have taken photographs of the bands of glyphs preserved on the narrow frontal faces (Plate II), and have made a tracing of the incised inscription on the upper face (Fig. 1).

Fig. 1.—Chinikihá: Portion of Incised Inscription upon Upper Surface of Stone Table.

Adjoining the north side of the ruined pyramid is an extensive palace with several courts. On one side of the main court there is a row of narrow entrances, which are arched over with triangular arches flattened at the top. ∩ These entrances, I think, did not lead to actual apartments, but only to a passageway by which chambers in the rear and at the sides may have been reached, while the horizontal stone roof formed an elevated passage to adjoining terraces.

Climbing over the ruins of the fallen chambers, which lie opposite the structure with the flattened triangular arches, we came to further remains of buildings and to a covered passageway, which must have led to chambers now filled with débris. Traces of painting (red scroll work) were still visible on the plastered walls of this passageway (or anteroom), but they had become so indistinct that it was impossible for me to copy the design.

Since the principal façades of this group of edifices, especially that of the temple, must have faced the west, I carefully searched the ground in front of it for sculptured stones, and found a small circular sacrificial table, and near it the fragments of a small stela, which had the figure of a man on one side and an inscription on the other. Unfortunately both sides of the stela were so much worn off by the rain that I could not photograph them. Whether the destruction of this stela is also to be imputed to the monteros and the fire which broke out at that time, it was useless to inquire. I will only remark that in almost all cases where a sculptured stela is dashed down by the accidental fall of a forest giant, the picture facing upward is destroyed, but the one turned downward is marvellously well-preserved. The only explanation I can give for the fact that both faces of this stela were worn off is, that some intruder out of curiosity had turned the fragments over and had then left them lying there.

This second group of edifices lies in the northeastern part of the city, and at a slight distance from it, but to the northeast there is a large truncated pyramid, which might prove of great interest to a future explorer able to undertake excavations on a more extended scale. Without wishing further to blame the honest woodcutters — who apologized to me for having meddled in archaeological matters by saying that they could not have foreseen that some time I should penetrate into these hidden corners — I must mention, however, to complete the matter, that one of the mozos found among these ruins a small sculptured stone in perfect preservation which, it is said, still showed some traces of colors, and that he had carried it off with the intention of selling it to one of the managers of La Reforma. But on the road — who knows where? — on thinking the matter over and being in doubt whether he should receive the hoped-for recompense of fifty pesos, and the stone being somewhat heavy, he hid it in the woods. At the time of my stay in La Reforma, this man was in far-off Tzendales; hence it was utterly impossible to find the stone, which may now be forever lost.

III.

CHÁNCALA.

Cháncala (tsánkalá) is the name of a plant with large leaves, the seed-pods of which contain small black balls, which, when pierced with holes, are used by the Indian women for necklaces. It is the *Heliconia* of the botanists.

At the end of January, 1898, leaving the larger part of my baggage at La Reforma, I went with my men to the waterfall of the Cháncala River to investigate a ruined city in that locality. The road was extremely miry and occasioned us much trouble. We passed first through a small rancho, and were courteously received by the occupant, who had lost his right hand while pressing sugar-cane. We crossed the Cháncala River about one league above the waterfall, where lie the crumbling huts of the abandoned montería, La Cuña. Hard by the waterfall — on the right bank — are also the huts of a former lumber-camp, El Chorro, and in the best of these we settled ourselves for the night. We were about seven leagues from La Reforma.

The ruined city is perhaps three kilometres to the south of these huts, but owing to the extremely dense vegetation, it was impossible to reach it by a direct route. Therefore, when we were ready the next morning, the guide whom we had obtained at La Reforma, preferred to follow the path leading down stream for a considerable distance and then, turning to the right, to go up hill by a very much overgrown wood-road. On our journey we passed several streams of water, clear as crystal, whose banks were gay with interesting flowers. Finally we came to some masonry which enclosed an artificial mound of earth, from which, however, the structures which had once surmounted it had entirely disappeared. In spite of the fact that we had successfully reached the ruined city we were seeking, the guide who had been sent with us became so discouraged, owing to the rank vegetation which obstructed all the former paths, that with all sorts of prevarications and lying pretexts he cowardly forsook us and returned to La Reforma. I quietly let the rascal go, as I had very capable men with me. We at once began to explore the forest in which the ruins lay in all directions. We found a considerable number of substructures, both large and small, heaps of ruins, etc. In the southwestern part of the town we climbed a high natural hill in the hope of finding the principal temple on its top. Indeed near the summit there were remains of terrace walls, and at the very top a small ruined pyramid indicated that a temple had formerly stood there. From this hill we were able to overlook, in a measure, the surrounding country, without however gaining an advantage thereby, on account of the exceedingly tall growth of the trees. The trunks of many of the trees were of extraordinary thickness and height. An especial object of wonder to me was a ceiba — *yāxché* (*yās-tse* = green stem) as the Mayas call it — of giant proportions.

In the northwestern part of the town we were first successful in discovering a temple, in a fairly good state of preservation, which crowned a small pyramid of six terraces. To make the satisfaction of my men complete, they shot a slender variety of monkey, a *mico*, so that we had no lack of meat. The front of the temple faced the west, and my men began carefully to cut down the vegetation on that side, while I drew the plan (Fig. 2).

A broad flight of steps, now of course partially in ruins, leads up to the platform of the pyramid. The latter, which is about nine metres high, is composed of six terraces, some of which are still distinctly visible. The entrance to the interior of the temple is two hundred and fifty centimetres wide, and formerly had wooden lintels, which were either torn out by ruthless hands or were destroyed by some other means. As a result, the corresponding pieces of the frieze and the vaulted ceiling have fallen down and the passage is obstructed. The interior of the temple is two hundred and thirty-three centimetres wide, three hundred and ninety long, and four hundred and sixty-three high, from the cemented floor to the truncation of the

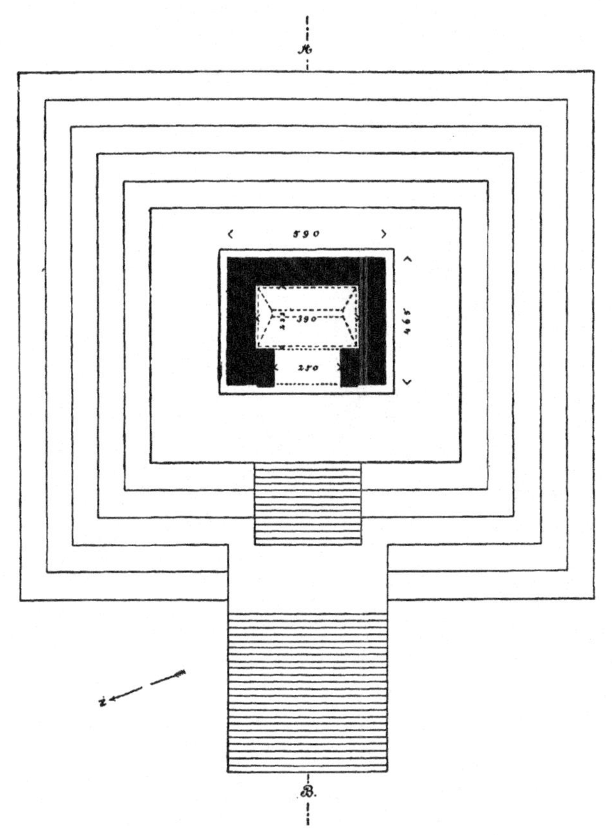

FIG. 2. — CHÁNCALA: PLAN OF TEMPLE AND SUBSTRUCTURE.

pointed arch of the vault, which at its base is separated from the face of the wall by a cornice. The walls of the room had evidently been covered over at different times with fine white stucco. Near the inner edges of the door jambs, both above and below, there is always a wall-ring hollowed out of a stone protruding from the masonry, which served to hold the wooden pegs of the mats or basket-work screens which covered the doorways.

The exterior of the temple is as follows: A stone bench, projecting about thirty centimetres, runs all around, forming a strong foundation.

The main surfaces of the wall are smooth, but on both sides of the entrance I could discern traces of a scrolled border; besides this, close below the projecting slabs of the cornice, along the entire façade, ran a red band of hieroglyphs, and below this another red band, which was intersected by the lintel. Even on the smooth surface of the front wall vestiges of red color were perceptible, so that it may be assumed that the entire front surface of the main wall, together with the edge of the door and the band of glyphs, was painted fiery red, with the exception of the small squares containing the hieroglyphs — of which only three are preserved — and these it seems

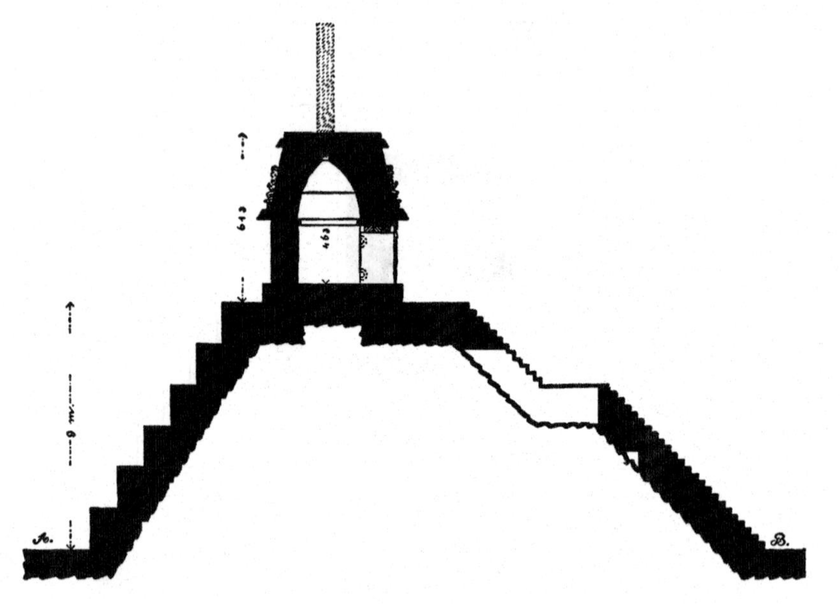

FIG. 3. — CHÁNCALA: CROSS-SECTION OF TEMPLE AND SUBSTRUCTURE.

to me were left white so that they might form a contrast to the red background. The glyphs did not form a closely consecutive series, but were separated by rather wide intervals. One of the little pictures shows two charming faces in profile, one placed half over the other, surrounded by some explanatory signs. The other two glyphs consist of tangled scrolls.

The frieze has a heavy cornice, composed of strongly projecting bevelled slabs, and above this lies a somewhat receding course of stone. The steeply sloping surfaces of the frieze were probably ornamented at the corners and at stated intervals with sitting figures in stucco, measuring about two-thirds of the height of the frieze (Fig. 3). Only the stones forming the bases of these figures are preserved, while the greater portion of the stucco has fallen off. The upper cornice of the frieze is like the lower, but less heavy.

I am sorry to say that it was no longer possible to tell whether the temple had been formerly crowned by an ornamental coping or not. The height of the exterior of the temple from the platform to the upper edge of the cornice, I calculated at about 6.13 metres. The length is about 5.90 metres and the breadth 4.65 metres.

On the third day we again returned to the ruined city to photograph the temple (Plate III), which was rendered very difficult by the unfavorable light. As a matter of course, we also explored the ground at the western side of the temple to see if we might not find a sacrificial altar, or a stela representing a god or marking a grave, but we searched in vain. This region of ruins is also variously traversed by brooks, whose water, ice-cold at this season, greatly refreshed us while we discussed our roast monkey and other provisions with a keen relish. All the streams are filled with edible snails, *Melania levíssima,* = *xot* (*šot*) of the Mayas. The shells of the dead snails are soon covered with a thick calcareous crust, which continually increases as the years go by, forming cones of various sizes until the uninitiated would hardly suspect that the resultant mass had once been a snail-shell. A day was also devoted to photographing the magnificent waterfall (Plate IV). In order to descend the steep walls of the ravine in front of this waterfall, we had to tie ropes to the trees. In this way alone were we able to accomplish the descent and to carry the photographic apparatus down uninjured. Setting up the camera on the rocks below, I took two photographs, one of which was very successful, in spite of the difficulty in harmonizing the dark trees with the blinding whiteness of the waterfall and the blue sky. Further on, below the waterfall, the river forces its way between high cliffs, affording a series of very picturesque scenes.

Having finished our task, we returned to La Reforma.

IV.

XUPÁ.

Xupá (*šupá*) = Brook of the Ants. In Yucatan the army ants are called *xulab* (*šulab*).

We left Reforma on the 4th of February, 1898, crossing the Chacamax in a cayuco and loading our animals on the left bank. We took the road to Palenque, and the first settlement we reached was the montería, La Nueva Esperanza, which had been recently established close to the left bank of the Chacamax. The proprietor, Don Luis Gónzali of Comalcalco, received us very kindly.

Sr. Gónzali was formerly in the employ of the firm of Romano, and directed the building of the road from La Reforma to Tzendales, which established the communication between two widely separated settlements. In this vast stretch of wilderness the workmen did not once encounter a ruined city; however, about eight leagues from Tzendales, at a point which the men called *Champa de San Pedro* (not far from the San Pedro River), during an excursion into the forest to the left of the road, Sr. Gónzali, accompanied by Rafael Naranjo, came upon a temple which crowned a small cerro (presumably a pyramidal substructure). As it was already late in the evening and these gentlemen and their mozos were obliged to hasten back, they made only a hurried inspection of the edifice. They remembered, however, that its ground plan showed a rectangular passage. ⊓ They also saw earthen vessels in the interior, but they did not attempt a further exploration of the ruined city, which is doubtless in the vicinity. I temporarily gave the name *Naranjo-Gónzali* to these ruins, which I hope may some day be explored. Furthermore, in connection with a land-survey which certain engineers made on the Lacanhá River (which runs parallel, so to speak, with the Usumatsintla, but in the opposite direction, flowing into the Lacantun), ruins were found to which I gave the name *Ruinas de Lacanhá*, though as yet I have been unable to undertake an expedition to them for lack of more definite information. Later on Sr. D. José Némecke — an experienced man in the lumber-business — told me that the edifice discovered by Gónzali forms part of the ruined city near the river Lacanhá, and that no other ruins exist in that region. I am inclined to agree with this opinion of Sr. Némecke.

On the following day we went to the rancho Sulusúm, belonging to Mr. German Koller, whom I fortunately met on the road and having interchanged greetings with him, I communicated to him my intention of visiting the ruins of Xupá from his rancho. We had formerly been acquainted, having met in 1877, when I visited the ruins of Palenque; Mr. Koller, therefore, consented most courteously to my plan, and promised to accompany me in person, as soon as he should return from a short trip which he was obliged to make at that moment.

About one and one-half leagues from Palenque, we turned aside to the left of the road and passing over the remains of a very ancient city, we soon came to the rancho picturesquely situated on the left bank of the Chacamax, where we were very kindly received by Mr. Koller's wife.

We remained here two days awaiting Mr. Koller's return, and employed the time in exploring the ruins in the neighborhood, which was the easier inasmuch as large milperias had been established here in recent years and the ruins therefore lay exposed in the abandoned stubble-fields. We did not succeed, however, in discovering a single sculptured stone; not even in the vicinity of what was once the principal temple, and which is now reduced to a moderately large heap of ruins. But in one place we found large gutter-tiles of baked clay deep in the ground.

Meanwhile Mr. Koller had returned, and on the 8th of February we left the rancho in his company, crossing the Chacamax at a little distance from the huts. Our path now led through the mountain spurs of this region, until, after travelling about two and one-half leagues, we reached the brook of Xupá. Here we found a small palmleaf hut, or champa, where my men unloaded the pack animals and put the camp in order, while I myself with Mr. Koller crossed the stream in search of the principal edifice of the ruined city, as Mr. Koller wished to return to his rancho on the same day. We succeeded in reaching this edifice, blazing the direction thither by cutting off branches, so that on the next day the thorough exploration might be carried on without interruption.

Our camp by that bubbling brook was very comfortable, but about midnight the piercing scream of a panther awoke us from our light slumbers. This animal is not directly dangerous to man, but its repeated shrill cry somewhat disconcerted my men, who were not exactly heroes. It seemed to have the same effect upon a troop of howling monkeys. They had enlivened the stillness of the night with their loud howling, but at the first cry of the panther they were struck dumb, and from this I inferred that the *Stentor niger* and the *Felis concolor* are not on good terms.

The ruins are situated on the right bank of the Xupá and are of considerable extent. Nearly all the buildings appear to have had great substructures built of good hewn stone. The superstructures are almost without exception in ruins, but in all directions there are massive substructures many of which are of considerable size. I have explored very nearly all the buildings and the ground in front of them for sculptured stones, but in vain. The principal temple, once a noble edifice crowning a large pyramidal substructure, alone still exhibits parts of rooms and remains of walls.

I therefore directed my attention chiefly to the examination of this building. The temple with its façade faces the east. On this side were the flights of stairs, the terraces forming broad steps, and apartments, now in ruins, adjoining the temple at its base, which were reached from the place in front of the temple. On the west side, on the other hand, the steps of the pyramid formed an ascent to a plateau (west terrace), and from this additional steps rose to the platform.

As the façade of the temple proper, the right wing, and the middle part are almost entirely in ruins, I had great difficulty in understanding the ground plan of the temple, but I finally discovered that it was similar to that of the three well-known temples of Palenque, — the Temple of the Trophy and the first and second Temples of the Cross, — which proves beyond all doubt that Xupá was very intimately connected with Palenque. Accordingly the temple consisted of a finely vaulted vestibule with four pillars (strips of walls) in front, whose corresponding three entrances were spanned by wooden beams, upon which rested the frieze ornamented with figures in stucco. A middle room and two small side rooms corresponded to the vestibule, and into the middle room the sanctuary proper was built, the longitudinal wall of which was adorned with very interesting groups of figures. In three points, however, the temple of Xupá differs from its Palenque model:

First, The vaulted ceilings of the side chambers at the rear do not run parallel with that of the vestibule, but at right angles to it.

Secondly, The sanctuary is more massive (thick-walled) in its construction.

Thirdly, The figures on the longitudinal wall of the sanctuary are not in bas-relief, but incised.

In consequence of the fall of the façade as well as of the vaulted ceiling of the middle room, the entrance to the sanctuary was entirely blocked and the sanctuary itself was buried beneath the ruins. Being thus hidden from sight, it might have been preserved to posterity, if a few years ago inquisitive treasure-seekers from the village of Palenque and the monterías on the Cháncala, suspecting a hollow space within this heap of stones, had not made an opening from above, or directly through the vaulted ceiling. These people had not sense enough to surmise that an entrance should be made from in front! When these vandals — using the opening they had made — had descended into the inner chamber, which was painted fiery red, they found that its longitudinal wall was faced with seven narrow stone slabs, on the smooth surfaces of which an extremely interesting group of figures had been incised in outlines drawn with masterly skill. The fact that the thin slabs, which were only forty to forty-five centimetres wide, did not appear to be too heavy for transportation, excited the avarice of these men. Accordingly they decided to pry them off and to sell them secretly. They went to work in a most brutal fashion to execute this decision. It may be assumed that the centre of the mural picture represented an altar (or possibly a cross), which occupied the three middle stones, while at the right and left stood male and female figures, perhaps four in all. As the central portion was incomprehensible to these rogues, it appeared to them of but little value, and they broke the slabs in pieces! I found their fragments scattered about on top of the debris, but I found it impossible to make anything out of them. The slabs with figures seeming to be the most valuable, they dragged them out, but not possessing the proper means of transportation to carry them home, they hid part of them on the slope of the pyramid and others farther off in the forest, who knows where? Only a single slab did these vandals leave on the wall, because, in trying to pry it off with their crowbars, they had knocked off the entire face of the personage represented on it. This figure represents a man of rank, wearing a high helmet with a feather ornament, a necklace, a breastplate of scales, etc. As the face has been entirely destroyed, this figure is worthless and I have made no drawing of it. I searched the terraces of the pyramid very thoroughly for the missing stones, and was fortunate enough to find one of them. This slab was ornamented with the outlines of a lovely female form, having a high and graceful head-dress, a pure Maya profile, a collar of net-work with an edge of beads, and a disk on the middle of the breast. Under her right arm she holds a small animal (bird?) prepared for a sacrificial gift. She wears the girdle with a mask in front and a St. Andrew's cross at the side, a skirt of net-work with bead fringe, etc. I have made a tracing of this single acquisition of my explorations (Fig. 4).

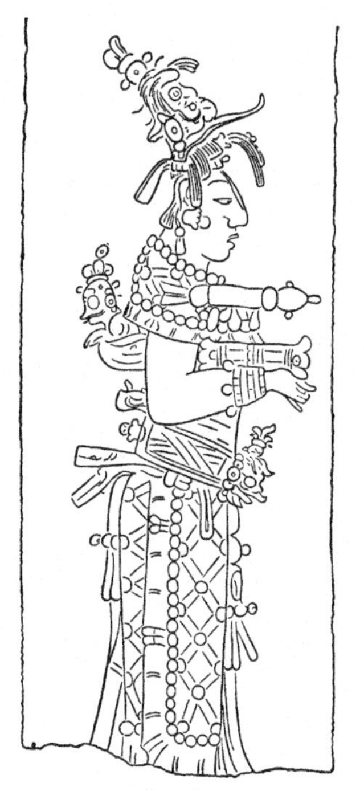

FIG. 4.—XUPÁ: INCISED CARVING UPON STONE SLAB, INNER CHAMBER OF TEMPLE. ⅛.

My annoyance at the ruthless destruction of the decorations of the sanctuary of the temple at Xupá will probably be shared by all Americanists. This crime was probably perpetrated somewhere about the year 1890, notwithstanding the local authorities of Palenque, or rather of El Salto de Agua, had repeated and strict injunctions from the central government to protect the ancient monuments.

It is probable that the temple was once crowned by an airy roof-comb of twofold character, erected on the roofs of the vaulted chambers, which was similar to that of the temples of Palenque. The entire structure viewed from the eastern environs must have been most imposing.

On the temple site itself I could discover no sacrificial altars or stelæ with figures of gods; I found only the remains of numerous smaller structures.

Before starting on the return journey from these ruins I made an excursion to the montería established on the Mistolhá by an American, McQueen. My object was in part to inquire of his men whether in their wanderings in this wilderness they had seen ruins, and in part to gratify my desire to photograph the magnificent waterfall formed by the river.

Mr. McQueen received me kindly and gave me a guide to the waterfall. As there had been heavy rains during the preceding days, we had difficulty in crossing the Mistolhá, in order to reach the waterfall from the right bank. The waterfall is about two leagues below the montería and is indeed a splendid sight. The boiling mass of water rushes down a wall of rock one hundred feet in height, piling up such vast masses of spray that it was well-nigh impossible to take a photograph. I finally succeeded, however, with great difficulty in taking one.

According to a statement of the men, "the petrifaction of a large antediluvian animal" is visible on a boulder when the water is low in the basin at the foot of the falls. An American told me, however, that this petrifaction was only about thirty centimetres long, and was a very distinct and pretty representation of a fish. While I was encamped near the waterfall all these rocks were under the water, and therefore I could not inspect the fossil.

The Mistolhá flows into the Baxcan, which in its turn is a tributary of the Rio de San Pedro Savana.

Having retraced our steps to the montería of Mr. McQueen, we rested there for a day, enjoying the agreeable society of that gentleman, and then we turned towards Sulusúm and Palenque.

V.

PETHÁ.

After exploring the route from Chinikihá to Palenque, I found it necessary to return to my headquarters in Tenosique to organize a second expedition, — this time for the exclusive purpose of rediscovering the long since forgotten Lake of Pethá. Having engaged new men and procured fresh provisions, in the middle of August, 1898, I went for the second time to the montería La Reforma, where I had left my luggage. The rainy season in the mean time had set in in full force, the forest paths were soaked, and all the rivers and brooks were swollen. Nevertheless, very fine weather might be expected even at this season.

The first part of the road, which has been built by the firm of Romano from La Reforma to Tzendales, running directly through the wilderness, is excessively bad, because the workmen found no firm, stony soil, but only black forest loam. This ground is so boggy throughout the entire year that not even those who laid out the road ventured to use it with their horses or mules. Each traveller, therefore, at the beginning of this road endeavors to take certain circuitous paths leading from abandoned lumber camps, and only strikes into the actual *camino de los Tzendales* at the Chocolhá. We too followed the general practice, and when on the 27th of August I was able to start from La Reforma with my men and mules, after crossing the Chinikihá we took the narrow forest trail to the abandoned montería of El Clavo, about three leagues from La Reforma, where the forsaken huts afforded us sufficient shelter from the rain during the night.

On the second day of our journey, in spite of the wretched, miry, and, at times, also mountainous paths, we reached the Chocolhá, where the neighboring monterías have a ferryman who carries the traveller over in a cayuco. This ferry is called La Culebra and is about five leagues from El Clavo. But about three kilometres before we reached the Chocolhá, we were obliged with much difficulty to ford the greatly swollen Chancalá, for there was no cayuco here. At La Culebra we found protection from the rain at night in an open hut, *un galeron*, on the left bank. The ferryman's hut was on the opposite bank.

On the morning of the 29th of August we crossed the Chocolhá with the help of a large cayuco, loaded our pack animals, and from this point took the road to Tzendales, which was in a wretched state besides being very mountainous. Finally we took a forest trail on the right, and late in the afternoon we reached the montería of Las Tinieblas, which had been recently established on the right bank of the upper Chocolhá and — as I had learned — was at that time the most advanced post for those who wished to reach the Lake of Pethá. The distance from Culebra to Tinieblas I estimated at five leagues.

Las Tinieblas is a branch of the great lumber enterprise of Troncoso Cilveti y Ca., who had recently begun the exploitation of the forests along the Chocolhá and whose privileges extend to the vicinity of the Lake of Pethá. After I had explained the object of my coming to the encargado of the montería, we agreed to send a messenger on the following day to the administrator of the concession, Mr. Cayetano Irigoyen, who was fortunately just then staying at the neighboring montería La Ilusion, and whom I had informed of my intention when I was in Tzendales. In due time I received the following courteous reply from Mr. Irigoyen:

Troncoso Cilveti y Ca.
Corte de Maderas preciosas.
Chiapas.

La Ilusion, Agosto 30 de 1898.

Señor Don Teoberto Maler,
Montería Las Tinieblas.

Muy Señor mio, — Correspondo con gusto á su atenta de hoy en lá que me pide un práctico para su excursión á la laguna Pethá.

Obsequiando sus deseos, irá mañana nuestro dependiente Francisco Guillen para acompañarlo, aunque sus conocimientos prácticos en esos lugares no son muy precisos, pero sí creo suficientes para llegar bien al punto deseado: pues las mensuras de los terrenos de esta casa, en cuya apertura estuvo él, se aproximan á unos pocos kilómetros de la laguna.

Deseando le sea satisfactoria su visita á estos desiertos me repito su affectísimo amigo y servidor

Cayetano Irigoyen.

Tinieblas is occasionally visited by neighboring Lacantuns, who sell to the employees beautiful bows and arrows, rare birds and other articles; and yet none of the people here had the least idea where the Lake of Pethá was situated or how the Indian settlements could be reached.

As was my custom, I closely questioned the men here whether in their search for trees or in hunting, they had ever found ruins. They declared unanimously that they had never seen a trace of ruins in the neighboring forests.

Mr. Guillen arrived on the 31st of August, and all the details of our projected expedition were discussed most thoroughly with him. As I was fully prepared, we were able to leave Tinieblas on the next day (September 1st). Our saddle and pack animals were, of course, left behind. There were six of us in all. We took with us only a small camera (9 × 12 cm.) and the most necessary provisions. In addition we were all armed.

Following a forest path, we came once more to the camino de los Tzendales and to the halting-place San Antonio, where a large galeron invited repose; but as this San Antonio is barely two leagues from Tinieblas, we continued our march and pitched our tent near a small brook about a league from El Espejito. On the road we met some men with a train of mules coming from Tzendales. They were also carrying with them some bound mozos, who had committed a horrible double murder at Tzendales.

At an early hour on September 2nd we reached the halting-place El Espejito, about four leagues from San Antonio. Here we decided to abandon the road to Tzendales, and turning to the right, we pushed forward into the forest in a southerly or southeasterly direction. Soon we had to ford a not insignificant tributary of the Chocolhá, and in doing so we took advantage of the lime-rock formations of the river bed at this spot. A few steps beyond we found to our great joy an Indian trail which led in exactly the same direction which we had intended to take. Convinced that this trail must lead somewhere, we followed it for two leagues over hills and ravines, coming finally to a pass on the upper Chocolhá (right bank), where, from all appearances, the Lacantuns were accustomed to cross the river.

At this spot the river, flowing over a great bed of lime rock, forms a small waterfall only about one and one-half metres high. In the dry season the Indians probably cross the river by walking on this ledge, but at present the river was so high that such a proceeding was out of the question. In the mean time we encamped on a terrace on the hither side, erecting a small palmleaf hut for the night. Then we felled several small trees of light wood, which we cut into six long pieces and fastened them firmly together by means of tough vines, *bejucos* (climbing plants). Having finished our small raft, we decided to attempt a crossing a little below the waterfall, at a place where the river forms large, deep pools.

One of my most skilful men, provided with a long pole and a large roll of bejucos, boldly leaped on to the raft and safely reached the other bank. The improvised bejuco rope was now firmly fastened to either shore.

I had bidden the man search carefully on the opposite bank to see whether the Indians had not concealed a small boat somewhere among the trees projecting into the water. Hardly had he touched the opposite bank when his joyful shout announced that he had found a fine new cayuco. He unfastened the boat, got into it, and brought it to our bank, abandoning the now useless raft to float down the river.

The cayuco had very recently been made from a *caoba* tree. We tied it firmly to a tree, lest it should be torn away during the night by the chance swelling of the stream. The finding of this cayuco was the second piece of good fortune that befell us on our expedition to Pethá.

There was now nothing further to do, and we cooked a fine *Crax rubra,* which we had killed on the way. It invariably rained at night.

On the morning of September 3d, after crossing and recrossing the river three times, the passage over the Chocolhá was completed. The little Indian boat was now fastened as securely as possible to the left bank, so that it might serve us on our return. At a distance of only two hundred paces from our crossing-place, we saw a well-built open champa, and a smaller one near by for cooking. Several pottery cooking-utensils lay around, and at a short distance we saw the clearing where the caoba had been felled and the cayuco had been made. Numerous hunter's trails ran in all directions from the hut, which was very confusing to us, but, true to our purpose to move always in a southerly or southeasterly direction, we chose the path which seemed to correspond best to that direction. The sequel proved that we had made a wise choice. We marched on uninterruptedly, crossing numerous brooks and also on the left a large tributary of the Chocolhá. The region became wilder and more mountainous, but we followed the path closely uphill and downhill, though it was often hardly discernible, convinced that it must lead somewhere. Towards noon, as we were already very tired, we made a short halt for rest and food. Then we pushed on again in spite of heavy showers of rain which drenched us to the skin. Finally we came to a small milpa established in the midst of the forest. This was the first sign that we were near an Indian settlement. The rain ceased. We proceeded cautiously. Descending the last declivity, suddenly a silvery expanse of water gleamed between the dark branches of the trees. A few steps further down, the path ended at the waters of the Lake of Pethá. Where the path ended three cayucos were fastened to the trees, and the oars belonging to them were found hidden in the branches. This was the third piece of good luck that had befallen us on our romantic expedition to Pethá. Indeed, of what advantage would it have been to us to have reached the lake without boats to navigate it! Fearing rain in the night, we went promptly to work to erect a large champa close to the water, covering it as well as we could with palmleaves and pieces of cloth. We also slung from tree to tree the hammocks which we had brought with us, and soon in grateful repose forgot the hardships of the day.

The distance from Chocolhá to the northern border of the Lake of Pethá was probably only five or six leagues, but as the Indian trail was very much overgrown, we had frequently to use our machetes to make our way through. It was near the close of the day. All was in order. I revelled in the enjoyment of the glorious panorama afforded by the lake, which here forms a large almost circular basin more than two kilometres in diameter. On the distant southern shore, opposite our camping-place, we saw quite a large waterfall plunging into the lake, the sound of which reached us from the distance. Low mountain ranges bordered the southern shore, and in the background towered the mighty crests of the Sierra Madre in what we supposed to be the direction of Ocotzinco.

Suddenly my men who were employed in cooking informed me that a cayuco was passing near the distant southern shore. I attentively looked in that direction, and just as the cayuco passed in front of the waterfall, I distinctly saw its black silhouette with two men standing erect thrown into bold relief against the white background. Soon after the cayuco vanished into one of the coves in that vicinity, the position of which we impressed upon our memories. This was our first sight of human beings, but the Indians on their part had not noticed us. I had the two best cayucos cleaned and all the seams very carefully calked with clay. The necessary oars — *canaletes*, as they are called here — were also made ready, and on Sunday, September 4th, we rowed for the first time on the lake in our small barks so fortunately acquired. There were only two men in each, while two remained in the camp (Plate V, 1, 2).

However lazy and shiftless the men of Tenosique may be in other respects, they display great aptitude on the water. It seems indeed as if rowing were the only occupation which they do not object to, for they perform all other labor with the greatest reluctance.

We crossed the lake in the direction of the waterfall, where we had seen the small boat disappear (Plate V, 5). We found at the right of the waterfall a small inlet hidden among the trees, to the bank of which several cayucos were fastened. We secured our boats here and followed a rather rocky trail inland. After travelling for about half an hour we came to a large milpa in which bananas, *papayos*, and sugar-cane were growing, in addition to very tall maize. At the end of the milpa we saw a group of houses, which we approached; but no one came to meet us, and there was no barking of dogs. The stillness of death prevailed on all sides. We entered the houses. There were two large ones intended for the main dwellings, which were surrounded by several small huts, which served for kitchens, sleeping-rooms, and shelters for small domestic animals. All were made entirely of poles roofed over with palmleaves. The two main houses and the adjacent huts were filled with household implements of every description, and gave a very complete idea of what the present Maya-Lacantun industry can produce in the way of articles for household use. Such an opportunity of examining all at once the entire domestic establishment, even to the slightest details, of this remarkable people, seemed to me not likely to occur again. I therefore at once set to work to examine everything, even the smallest object, directing my attention particularly to finding utensils that should display drawings which might be regarded as writing, since my many friends in Europe and America are especially interested in this particular question. Many cooking-utensils and water-jars, *çazuelas y cántaros*, lay scattered around on the floor of the huts and also on the ground outside. Everything was in great disorder, as if the inhabitants had suddenly forsaken their possessions. The cooking-vessels and pots resembled in shape those of the Indians of Yucatan and Tabasco, and were of dark gray-brown clay. The water-jars, *cántaros*, were of superior workmanship and were made of lighter, whitish-gray clay, and, strange to say, all were of the strongly bulging shape, which is generally considered peculiar to Spanish-African jars. Many had two handles near the neck, but some had only one handle and a small projecting animal head served the purpose of the other. Aside from the animal heads, none of this pottery had any designs whatever. There was a large grinding-stone, *metlatl*, on a platform which rested on pegs, and several smaller ones stood near by. Several large nets, which were filled with *calabaza* bowls, *xicalli* (Fig. 5), for drinking *potzol* and *balché*, hung on the rafters of the main houses; some of these were adorned with pretty incised designs (Figs. 6, 7), but there was nothing of a hieroglyphic

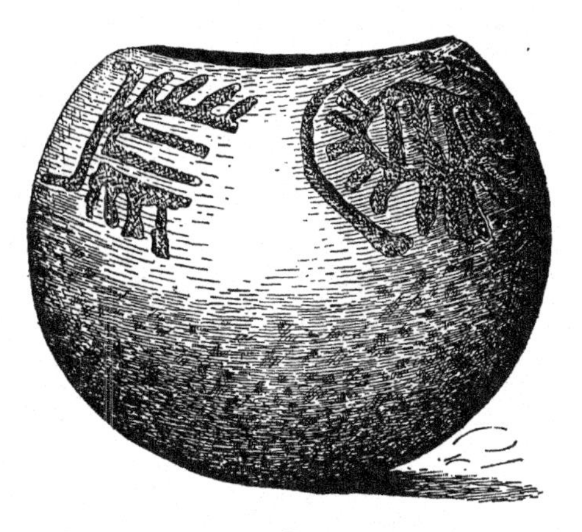

FIG. 5.—CALABASH DRINKING-VESSEL. ½.

FIG. 6.—INCISED DESIGN UPON CALABASH DRINKING-VESSEL.

character. The smoke had colored these vessels a beautiful dark-brown. From the rafters also hung bundles of tobacco leaves, which were most carefully wrapped in banana leaves. My men could not resist the temptation of taking a few of these for their own use. Several bows and arrows and other small trifles lay on the timbers at the base of the roof or hung on the vertical poles of the walls. In various gourds which I examined I found tree-resin, wax, aromatic herbs, seed-corn, lime, points of flint for arrows, and even alligator teeth, which were probably intended for the necklaces of the women, etc. Small spindles with cotton threads, small wooden spoons, tufts of feathers, and skulls of peccaries, deer, and apes were also stuck between the poles. There were even some billets of pitch-pine, *ocotl*, which must have been brought from a distance, for there are no pine-trees in the neighborhood of Pethá. In one of the small open huts hung a large gourd, which served for a bee-hive. It had a small hole on one side through which the bees passed in and out. My attention was attracted by some bird-cages, prettily plaited of a fine kind of bejuco, pear-shaped and having little trap-doors, and also by other baskets of simple but pretty shape. Of the different skins of small mammals, a yellowish one with brown spots seemed to me especially interesting, inasmuch as I had no knowledge of the little creature to which it belonged. Against the wall of the largest hut there was a wide board resting on pegs, which held a dozen of those well-known incense vessels each of which has the face of a god in front (Fig. 8). The majority of these were much larger than those which I had once found in the temples of Yaxchilan, but were less graceful and so completely covered with copal, *chapopotl*, burned quite black, that their shape was hardly recognizable. Knowing how unwilling the Lacantuns are that a stranger should approach their gods, I improved this opportunity to take the incense vessels for a moment out of the dark hut, and because they were so black, directly into the sunlight, in order to photograph them with my camera (Plate VI, 6) before we should be surprised by Indians who might come this way. When

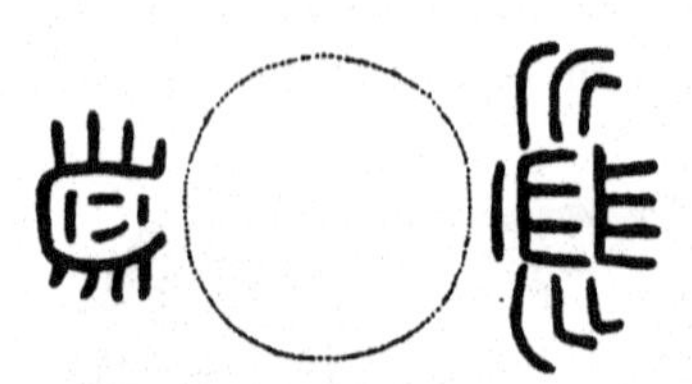

FIG. 7.—INCISED DESIGN UPON CALABASH DRINKING-VESSEL.

FIG. 8.—INCENSE BURNER OF TERRA COTTA. ½.

I had photographed them, I quickly put the vessels back in their places. Luxuriantly tall maize surrounded the huts, but there was a space left in which bloomed the beautiful yellow *Simpalxochitl* and the *Espuelas* — red dotted with white. There was also a little bed of *Yerba buena*.

Having thoroughly explored the huts, we intended to continue our journey in the hope of finding inhabited dwellings; but unfortunately the paths branched off in such a manner and were so ill-defined that we were puzzled which way to turn. We therefore decided to return to our camping-place, but not without taking a small supply of young maize ears, *elotl*, which, when boiled with salt, are an agreeable vegetable. As payment we left a mirror and a red silk handkerchief by the incense vessels. And as we crossed a large ant hill of yellow earth, I made several distinct impressions upon it with my shoes, thinking that if the Indians should come this way they would doubtless notice that strangers had been here and would wish to have intercourse with them. Once more embarked in our frail crafts, we visited the waterfall and slowly rowed past the small islands in this part of the lake, to our camp, where those guarding it had in the mean time somewhat improved the huts and cooked our evening meal.

On September 5th we undertook a thorough exploration of the lake in all directions. This time taking the right hand, that is, following the northern shore, we came to a canal overhung by trees, through which we pushed our way as well as we could. It led to an extremely picturesque, large western basin, a long narrow arm of which branches off in a northwesterly direction (Plate V, 6). This part of the lake is also surrounded on all sides by mountains. The most beautiful vegetation extends close to the water's edge, while in several places perpendicular cliffs rise to a height of twenty to thirty metres (Plate V, 3). We rowed all round this extension, especially examining the cliffs to see if they might not display pictorial representations of some kind. The indigenous vegetation developed on these often fantastically piled up rocks is of special interest. Many of the rarest orchids, bromelia- and agave-varieties, which are seldom met with elsewhere, were here just now at the height of their gorgeous bloom. After the exploration of this extension, we passed back into the transverse arm, which is also diversified by cliffs and islets, in order directly to enter a larger western or southwestern extension, which we likewise explored to its end. I had brought my little camera with me to take small views of the most beautiful spots, although convinced that it is impossible for photography alone to convey an adequate idea of the incomparable, ever-varying beauty of these sheets of water set in vegetation untouched by the hand of man. Small flocks of black aquatic birds, which my men called *cuervos de agua* (water-ravens), were stirred up here and there by the approach of our cayucos. Strange to say, we did not see a single duck or other species of water-fowl. Probably the birds stay away during the rainy season, because the lake has no beach; but I think it probable that ducks, herons, and pelicans frequent the lake in the dry season when the water has fallen perhaps full five metres and large portions of the shore are above water. We found the water very deep everywhere, and therefore used only oars and never poles. Returning from the southwest arm, we skirted the southern shore and the inlets on that side, and came to an exceedingly beautiful southern passage, which led back to the main or large eastern basin. Along this passage — on our left as we passed through — we again saw great cliffs rising perpendicularly from the water. These we also investigated in the hope of finding pictorial representations, and to our great joy we discovered three separate large pictures. The central picture appeared to me to be the most interesting and the best preserved. At a height of one and one-half metres above the surface of the water (in September) a drawing was visible executed in bold black lines, which I conceived to be the representation of the jaws of a monster (the eye was especially distinct) in the act of swallowing a man head foremost.

Fig. 9. — Lake Pethá: Rock Painting. $\frac{1}{8}$.

On the right (from the beholder) a smaller grotesque face develops out of the upper scrollwork, and on the left or at the back the head of the monster terminates in plumage (Fig. 9). The drawing is fifty-two centimetres high and fifty-seven wide. About one metre above this picture a diminutive man (about forty centimetres in height) is very crudely painted, also in black. Further up, a little to the right, are daubed large red hands (Fig. 10).

Fig. 10. — Lake Pethá: Rock Painting. $\frac{1}{8}$.

At the right of the central picture, in spite of the washing away by torrents of rain and the luxuriant vegetation, three and one-half metres above the surface of the water, we could discern the picture of a yellowish foot on a red ground (that is, a picture of the sole of the foot, with the toes pointing upward), and above this in red outlines on a yellowish ground an overturned pot (?) covered with red dots, from the lower edge of which project four comblike droppings. This little picture most resembles certain perforated vessels in which the women wash the maize, which has been soaked in lime water. There are several more red hands above the perforated pot and the foot at a distance of about seven metres above the surface of the water. Is it possible that this picture on the rock indicates the grave of a woman?

This simple symbolic picture may be interpreted thus: The footprint may indicate that the beloved woman has gone "upward." The overturned washing-pot probably shows that she never again will go to the river to wash out her *nixtamal* (softened maize), to make *tortillas* for her husband and children. . . . The red hands raised toward the sky may indicate the last greetings of those she left mourning on earth, when she ascended to celestial regions.

The representation at the left of the central picture is composed of large, broad red stripes, which run high up on the cliff, mostly in vertical lines and form large scrolls here and there. There are also two white or light yellow hands recognizable on a red ground, and adjoining this there is also a series of black lines, which, however, have become very indistinct.

After we had passed through the strait of the picture-rocks, with its poetic beauty, we turned into a bay on the southern shore where a second waterfall, shaded by tall trees, plunges foaming over the rocks into the lake. Then — as night was already approaching — we crossed the large eastern basin to our camp on the northern shore, where in the mean time our meal had been prepared, and we soon resigned ourselves to calm repose. The fact that we had explored this glorious lake even to its remotest corner without the aid of the Indians and without arousing the suspicion of these people, usually so crafty, and that, in addition, we had made use of their own cayucos, was a source of great astonishment to us. It seemed like a dream!

The entire length of the lake from the eastern margin of its large round basin to the extreme end of its western ramifications we estimated at six or seven kilometres. The diameter of the round basin, to which its name Pet-há, = *Agua circular*, refers, may be two kilometres, while the width of the western arms varies from two hundred to four hundred metres. We found the water of such great depth everywhere that steamships could easily sail on this lake, probably even in the dry season, when the water doubtless falls about five metres.

In the forenoon of September 6th we went again to the *Roca de las Pinturas*. I took some tracing paper with me in order to make a tracing of the well-preserved black drawings. A large *kommehen* (wood-destroying insect larvæ) nest, which was attached to the cliff below the drawing, we cut to pieces with our machetes. Having thus cleared the drawing, I fastened over it with small pieces of wax a large sheet of the transparent paper, and standing on a projecting rock, as best I could, I proceeded to make the tracing. Scarcely had I finished this somewhat trying task when my men told me that an Indian boat was coming toward us. I told the men to quietly await its arrival. I should have preferred not to encounter the Indians at the picture rocks, but there was not time to go elsewhere, and therefore I seated myself on the projecting rock to wait for the cayuco, which was not within my circle of vision. Suddenly the cayuco came around the rocks, and our friendly calls soon brought it alongside of our own. In it were a man, his wife, an infant, and two older children. Hardly had the man noticed that I was standing directly under the picture on the rock than, exhibiting signs of extreme terror, he called out to me in broken Spanish, "No hombre — quítate de ahi — es mi santo — es el Cristo-Maria de nosotros — cuidado hombre — te come el tigre — vámonos hombre — por eso mucha agua por el mal corazon de mi santo — por eso muy crecidos los rios y la laguna — vámonos — vámonos."

I pacified the man as well as I could, assuring him that we too held this "saint" in great veneration, and had brought him a small offering, so that he would grant us fine weather and abundant maize. After this I stepped into my cayuco, gave my hand to the man and asked him his name. Chankin, — *chichan*, abbreviated *chan* (*tšitšan, tšan*) = small; *kin* (*k'in*) = sun, priest, — he answered. Then I explained to him that we had come to see the lake and to visit his countrymen who were living in its vicinity, and also that we would like to purchase a few pretty things as well as food of them, for which purpose we had brought with us useful articles: knives, fish-hooks, handkerchiefs, mirrors, and salt, of which they never have a sufficient supply. On telling him that in our search for their dwellings we had come across a large group of houses full of all kinds of utensils, but without inmates, Chankin replied that the houses were those of his brother who had died recently. And what did he die of? "Quien sabe, Señor? — Por el mal corazon de su santo," the man answered angrily.

Chankin, who had learned a little Spanish in his frequent intercourse with the neighboring monterías, was a robust man in middle life, and was dressed in a shirt-like garment of coarse cotton. Long raven-black hair surrounded his beardless face, which was of a genuine Indian cast. His wife was of smaller frame, and was also dressed in cotton; her face and arms were badly bitten by flies. A fine set of bow and arrows wrapped in bark lay on the bottom of the cayuco. I asked the Indian to sell them to me, which he did for two pesos.

We rowed now to the landing-place on the south shore, where we fastened the boats. I was firmly resolved not to lose sight of the man at any price, for otherwise we might forever miss the opportunity of coming in contact with the Indian settlements of Pethá.

Chankin first took a path to the large waterfall. The river, which was very full at this season, rushed with tremendous force downward over terraced rocks into the lake. Our Indian took his way unconcernedly through the midst of this mass of water. I had had a stout walking-stick cut for myself, and there was nothing for me to do but to follow the man or to stay behind. Bracing myself firmly with my staff against the rocks, I too walked through the waterfall in extreme danger of being hurled into the foaming depths by the impetus of the rushing water. Taking off their shoes, three of my men followed very reluctantly. We then went on over desperately rough trails, soon reaching the same river (as I have reason to suppose) at a spot where it was spanned by the long and thick trunk of a tree, which at this time was about eighty centimetres below the surface of the water. At this place the river was several metres deep and impassable; so our Indian went straight over the smooth tree-trunk, in doing which the prehensile power of his toes was of great advantage to him. By the aid of a long pole in one hand and a shorter staff in the other, I succeeded with extreme difficulty in crossing. My men also made their way across by the aid of poles. Soon we had to cross the river for a third time, and again on the long and thick trunk of a tree, which this time, by way of variety, was suspended high above the water. We also successfully passed through this third and last Orphean ordeal to which Chankin subjected us.

On our way, however, between the first and second tree-bridges, we had caught glimpses among the trees on our right of "the dead brother's" large milpa, and I told my grumbling men that we should under no conditions go back over the frightful path by which Chankin had brought us, but that on our return we would clear a path to this milpa and then return to our landing-place by the trail we already knew.

After crossing the river for the third time, the path improved. We might have travelled about an hour, when we heard the barking of dogs and the hollow sound of conch-shells, *Strombus gigas*, with which the Indians greeted our arrival. The forest opened. We entered a milpa of tall and luxuriant maize, and from its group of huts Chankin's brother-in-law, *el suegro*, named Māx (*mās*) came to meet us surrounded by other Indians, including women and children. I saluted Māx, and explained my purpose in coming, while Chankin reported to him in Maya all the circumstances under which he had found us, so that I had no doubt that Chankin had been despatched to reconnoitre, purposely taking with him his wife and little children to cover his intentions.

Māx was not at all overjoyed at our arrival, but resigned himself to the inevitable. He promised us provisions — maize bread, *potsol*, *māxcal*, etc. — for the next day, when I was to visit him again with my men. For the present I found myself compelled to return as quickly as possible to the camp, as the day was near its end and we were threatened with a downpour of rain. We therefore took our leave, and lost no time in reaching the nearest tree-bridge. We notched the slippery surface of the trunk with our machetes, so that this passage lost much of its peril. Then, after reaching the point which brought us in line with the dead brother's milpa, we cut our way directly through the forest and without much difficulty reached the abandoned group of huts. Before we continued our journey, however, I permitted my men to take an abundant supply of ears of maize, bananas, and sugar-cane to punish the fellow who had dragged us over waterfalls and tree-trunks to his *suegro.*

Amid a light shower of rain we reached the landing-place. The last rays of the sun disappearing behind the mountains lighted us as we rowed over the mirror-like surface of the beautiful lake to our camp, where those who had been left behind had spent the day not without anxiety on our account. Of course my companions never wearied of recounting to their comrades all the experiences of this day. Each one considered himself a hero.

On the next day (September 7th), leaving but a single man to guard the camp, we all crossed the lake to visit Māx and his associates. We intended to take our noon meal there, in order to have leisure to observe the habits and customs of the Indians and to take some small photographs. After crossing the tree bridge we succeeded in killing a black crax.

As we neared the huts we heard the hollow, somewhat weird sound of the conch-shells with which Māx and his associates celebrated our coming. I greeted Māx and the assembled Indians cordially, explaining to them that we would like to spend the day with them, and as we had shot a *kambul,* would they lend us a vessel in which to cook it? Upon this one of the women brought us a large pot, and my men began to prepare the bird.

Then I told the Indians that I had brought them a few presents, articles which might be useful to them in their remote forests, and I at once proceeded to distribute the salt among the men who were present. Each one received a gourd-bowl full. I also gave each man a large knife and several kinds of fish-hooks. As for the women and girls, they received gay silk and cotton kerchiefs, as well as silver ear-pendants and pretty mirrors.

Although this people, so simple in its wants, is incapable of genuine joy, a certain feeling of general satisfaction, nevertheless, became evident among them. Meanwhile I had set up the small camera in order to take a few photographs before this pleasant mood should vanish. As my brightly varnished camera with its brass mountings was a pretty sight when set up on its slender tripod, the people were not at all frightened by this magic box. I succeeded in taking several photographs, which in spite of their small size (9 × 12 cm.) give a distinct picture of the features and dress of the men, women, and children (Plate VI, 3, 4, 5).

The men wear an ample shirt-like garment, of strong, somewhat coarse cotton material, which reaches down to the calves of their legs; but on their hunting expeditions or on journeys they wear a garment of extra-coarse fleecy material. The women wear an undergarment which reaches from the hips down over the calves of their legs, and the shirt-like upper garment falls over this. Each woman is adorned with a thick bunch of necklaces or rather strings of seeds. They are made of hard, usually black, seeds mixed with cylindrical bones, teeth, small snail-shells, or whatever else they can obtain.

The uncut hair of the men falls about their faces, which sometimes gives them a wild and leonine aspect. The women part their hair in the middle, exactly like European women, and at the end of the braid they fasten a tuft of gay bird-feathers, wings, and breasts. All the women have their ear-lobes pierced; so they could delightedly insert the ear-rings (of English manufacture) themselves or confidingly allow me to insert them. Neither men nor women seemed to wear shoes of any kind.

Māx's premises consisted of a large main hut, where he lived with his wives and children. This was surrounded by four smaller, half-open huts, some intended for cooking, and some for the accommodation of guests, and one was devoted exclusively to the incense vessels with faces of gods.

Here also was an abundance of cooking-vessels and implements of every sort, and the inmates had hammocks made of agave cord for sleeping at night and also for resting by day. The hammocks of the Lacantuns are very different from those which are used elsewhere in Mexico. They do not consist of mesh-work, but a system of cross cords holds the lengthwise cords together. They are also shorter than the Mexican ones, but are broad enough. The people do not make their things for sale, but only for their own use, so that it was utterly impossible for me to obtain one of their very prettily made hammocks.

The wooden implement with which the women weave the cotton cloth, *la manta*, is also interesting. An old woman was at work on a piece of material, and I wanted to buy the implement together with the partly finished web, but she obstinately refused to sell it. The women, however, gave me some of their seed necklaces as mementos, and I requested the men to bring a few of their beautifully made bows and arrows to my camp, promising to pay well for them.

The bows (Fig. 11) are usually made of *guayacan*, or *xibé*, or else of *chicozapote*. The length of the men's bows varies from one hundred and fifty to one hundred and seventy centimetres, that of the larger boys from one hundred and twenty-five to one hundred and thirty-five centimetres. All the bows are thicker towards the middle and taper very much toward the ends. Each end is firmly wound with a small cord, which is covered with resin, but the horns themselves are left free to receive the end loops of the bow-string, which is made of an agave cord, the windings of the small cord preventing the string from slipping when the bow is drawn. The bows are apparently straight, but on closer examination they are found to be very slightly curved. In using one of these bows, the rule must be followed of drawing the bow not — as one would be inclined to do — in the direction of the curve, in which case it would very easily break, but always in the opposite direction, that is to say, on the side of the outward curve (convex side). The Indians usually hold the bow horizontally before shooting, and only at the moment of aiming and of shooting is it placed in a perpendicular position. The arrows are only a little shorter than the bow. They are of different kinds, according to the game to be shot, but all, excepting the bird bolts, have this in common: the forward part, corresponding to about a third of the length of the arrow, consists of a cylindrical or a square rod of hard wood, which is deeply inserted in the reed shaft, *carrizo* or *caña brava,* and firmly lashed at the place of insertion and also at the invisible lower end. The reed shaft, which forms two-thirds of the length of the arrow, has at its butt the notch for receiving the string, and on both sides of the notch there is a feather, which is firmly bound at its upper and lower ends to the shaft, with twine smeared with black resin. If too broad, the feathers are cut out about the centre. The little hard-wood rods simply end in sharp points, which suffice for killing fish and small birds, or else flint-heads, varying in size, are inserted, and these are also firmly lashed at the place of insertion with cords covered as usual with black gum. The arrows, which are intended for killing monkeys, have the forward piece of hard wood deeply barbed, so that the animal cannot shake off or pull out the arrow. Lastly, the arrows which are intended to stun a bird only for the time being, so that it can be caught unhurt, have a little conical piece of wood in place of a flint head.

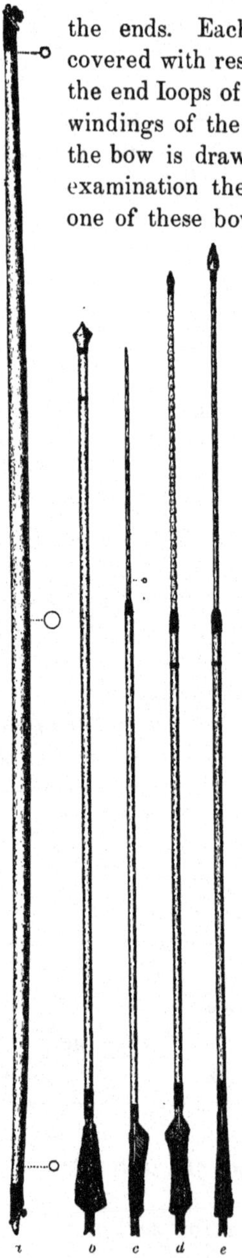

FIG. 11. — BOW AND ARROWS, LACANTUN INDIANS.

a, bow: *b*, bird bolt: *c*, wooden-pointed arrow for small game; *d*, stone-pointed monkey arrow; *e*, stone-pointed arrow for large game. 1/8.

The bow is bound up with the arrows, and the

bundle is protected by a covering of bark (*majahua*, as it is called in Tabasco) which is usually stripped from young ceiba-trees. The art of cleaving flint into thin layers has been preserved up to the present day by this secluded little nation. It appears that in some cases the cleaving is facilitated by previously heating the stone red-hot, but this is not always done. The cleaving is effected by means of a piece of deer-horn, especially prepared for this purpose, and by means of this elastic medium the blow of the mallet is

FIG. 12.—PACKAGE OF FLINT FLAKES, FROM WHICH ARROW-POINTS ARE MADE. ⅜.

transferred to the edge of the stone. The layers thus obtained (Figs. 12, 13) then receive the desired shape and an edge (Fig. 14), by means of a piece of an old knife (now made of iron). Inasmuch as the Indians also find many discarded bottles in the abandoned monterías, they use the glass of these bottles in place of flint. They make the arrow-points of this broken glass, which does not admit of cleaving.

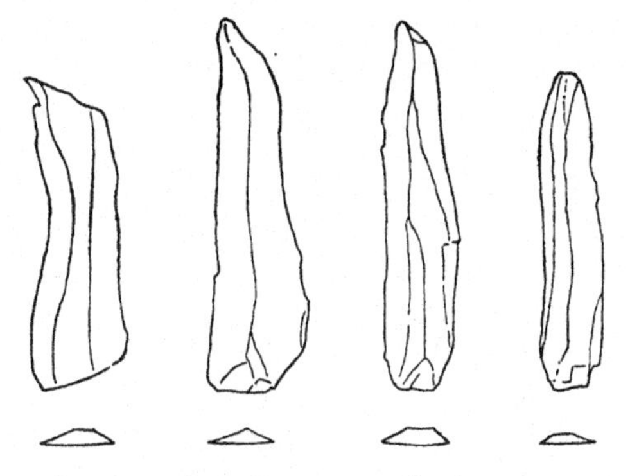

FIG. 13.—FLINT FLAKES FOR CHIPPING INTO ARROW-POINTS. ⅜.

There were only a few domestic animals to be seen on Māx's premises. The only mammals were dogs, which are always tied up, and belong to the present modern breed. Among the birds I noticed the large green parrots with blue heads, which occur exclusively in these forests. They are therefore called *los loros de los Lacandones* or *loros palencanos*. There were also several specimens of a beautiful small *Coturnix* species, called *bolonchac*, confined in small bejuco cages.

It is hardly to be expected that a remnant of those ancient breeds of dogs — *Techichi*, *Xoloitscuintli*, *Itscuintepotsotli* — should still be preserved among the Lacantuns. All the lumbermen who had come in contact with these Indians had seen only dogs of the same breed as those found everywhere in Mexico.

Hoping to throw light upon the still more important question as to the kind of pictorial representations still made by these Indians and whether they are of a hieroglyphic character, I looked about me very carefully in Māx's huts, but of course without exciting the suspicion of the people. I regret to say that nothing bearing upon this matter could be found. The fact that the Indians of Pethá live so scattered that each family is about one league (or an hour's journey) from the other adds much to the difficulty of solving this question. It would be necessary to ascertain whether these people are anywhere grouped in villages, for in that case there would be more prospect of obtaining specimens of drawings.

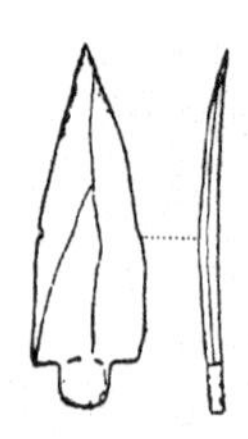

Fig. 14. — Flint Arrow-point, Lacantun Indians. ⅝.

In the mean time my men had deliciously prepared the crax, and the women supplied us with the necessary tortillas, which, made of new maize and half roasted, were especially palatable. At my special request, which I had also made on the preceding evening, they brought us large gourds full of balché (*baltšé*), a refreshing beverage made from the bark of a tree.

While we were satisfying our hunger with this food and drinking with it the national drink, balché, the men, having adorned their heads with bands dyed pink with chacavanté, withdrew into the huts containing the incense-vessels, to pray. The prayer consisted of monotonous, unintelligible cries, its purpose doubtless being to entreat the gods not to regard with anger the reception of strangers, and to avert any evil consequences that might arise from our visit. The women took no part in this religious ceremony.

At last the time came for us to depart, and we accordingly took leave of Māx and the other Indians. Before doing so, however, I administered to a young girl very ill with fever a small dose of quinine, which she took tearfully. To an older woman covered with ulcers (elephantiasis?) we could only recommend a draught which she could make herself of the sarsaparilla occurring in that region. With these exceptions the people were all in good health.

We remained four days more (September 8th, 9th, 10th, and 11th) on the shore of that beautiful lake, over whose waters we never grew weary of rowing. The Indians made us several visits, bringing us food and enabling us to buy of them several additional sets of their handsome bows and arrows.

Māx, whose name means "howling-monkey" (*Stentor niger*), was not a frank, kindly-disposed man. He very evidently exercised a certain repressing influence over the others, who showed much greater openness in their intercourse with us when Māx was not present, and willingly gave me all the information I desired.

I questioned the people very closely as to whether they knew of any ruins in the forests of this region. Unfortunately, absolute ignorance seemed to prevail among them in regard to the matter. Indeed, I had already convinced myself of the fact that cities built of stone had never existed in the neighborhood of Pethá. I only learned that at no great distance there were other smaller lakes: Hopethá to the southeast; the lake called Sib to the southwest, and between Pethá and Tinieblas another called Chichan-pethá, or "little round water."

To my question as to how many kinds of fish were to be found in the lake of Pethá, they answered five,—

1. Lú = el pezcado bobo, bagre.
2. Sohóm = una especia de mojarra.
3. Sactan = "sardina" (sactan = white-colored).
4. Chaclau = mulula of the Spaniards (chacil-au? [tšakil-au?] = with red dots, or red collar).
5. Dsibal, said to be quite a large fish (dsibal means "marking").

During the last days of our stay Heaven favored us with the most glorious weather. On the 12th of September we began our return march, without however taking leave of our Lacantun friends, since they had expressed their intention of accompanying us as far as Tinieblas. Arrived at the Paso del Chocolhá, we made ourselves comfortable in the large champa belonging to the Indians, who likewise arrived toward evening. We had killed another crax, and the Indians immediately after their arrival had very dexterously caught some fish, so that we had plenty of food. In addition, Māx had made me a present of a gourd full of honey.

One of the Indians, while he was cooking the fish, became confidential and said to me in broken Maya-Spanish: "I am sorry that you did not come also to my house — that you only went to see Māx, where I could not serve you. I too have maize at my house — you should have wanted for nothing at my house. Now that your heart is friendly towards me, I will tell you — that I also have a wife. Since you gave pretty ear-rings to all the women, but not to my wife — because she was not there — I will now ask you to give me a pair of ear-rings for my wife — that her heart may be made glad!"

I was very glad to learn, in this way, that the things I had given the people had evidently pleased them. Of course I picked out a pretty pair of ear-rings from what was left, and added a red silk handkerchief to make glad the wife of so excellent a husband.

There was a tremendously heavy fall of rain during the night, but early in the morning we succeeded in crossing the Chocolhá by means of the cayuco. Allowing ourselves but little time for rest, in spite of the soaked condition of the trails, we arrived late in the afternoon at Tinieblas, where the people regarded us with great respect and thought it wonderful that we, coming from a distance in the middle of the rainy season, had found the lake which they had never even seen.

The Indians made various purchases in the montería, and the very next day returned to their wilderness. We rested a day, and then set out on our return to La Reforma, where, when at last we arrived, we were, as always, most courteously received by Mr. Molina and the other gentlemen.

Here I dismissed my men from Tenosique, who had shown discontent during the whole expedition, and accepted Mr. Molina's kind invitation to go down the Chacamáx in one of the cayucos of the firm of Romano, as far as the Usumatsintla and to Montecristo, lying just below the confluence of the two rivers. Thence the return by steamer to my little house at our station in Tenosique offered no further difficulties.

VI.

PIEDRAS NEGRAS.*

After I had traversed the entire peninsula of Yucatan in 1895 and had rested in Flores — the ancient Peten-Itza — I took the route to the upper Usumatsintla by way of Sacluc, in order to return to Mérida by water *via* Tenosique and Cármen. Accordingly I came down from El Paso Real in a cayuco as far as the ruins of Yāxchilan, but from that point, owing to dangerous rapids, I was obliged once more to make use of forest trails in order to reach Tenosique, whence the journey to the sea was easily accomplished.

On the way, while spending the night at the montería El Cayo (on the left shore of the Usumatsintla) I made inquiries of the *Encargado*, Don Tránsito Mejenes, and of his people as to whether ruins of any kind whatever had been met with in the forests of this region, and I was successful in gaining information regarding the sites of several ruined cities, of which Piedras Negras proved to be the most important.

The distance from El Cayo to Tenosique is reckoned at twenty Mexican leagues. The first five bring one to the site of the ruins, where, until recently, there had been a montería under the management of Sr. D. Emiliano Palma, who by this time, however, had gone deeper into the forest with his men.

* For plan of the ruins see Plate XXXIII.

As it is impossible to undertake any serious explorations without having previously engaged some men and procured the necessary provisions, I contented myself for the time being with the information I had gathered, and passed by the ruins without inspecting them, fully determined to organize an expedition thither, as soon as I arrived in Tenosique.

On the 23d of July, 1895, I reached Tenosique in safety, and could then say that the most difficult part of my great journey of exploration had been overcome. I succeeded in coming to an agreement with a certain Luciano Sanchez, who was the owner of pack-animals and had several men at his disposal. He expressed his willingness to accompany me with three men and the necessary animals. I was to pay one peso a day for each man and each beast and to maintain them. Owing to the wood-cutting establishments in the neighborhood, which absorb all the available men, wages are very high in Tenosique. But as Sanchez and his men showed a willing disposition and behaved well, I did not regret paying them high wages. On the 12th of August our arrangements were completed and we left Tenosique.

For about two leagues our way led us through savánas adorned with numerous *nantsin*-trees, which were just unfolding the splendor of their yellow blossoms. This meadow-land comes to an end not far from the little river Polevá, which, in spite of its apparent insignificance, is regarded with much apprehension, because it often rises suddenly to such a height that it can be crossed only with great difficulty, or not at all. Afterward the trail runs mostly over low mountain ranges, where it is shaded by high forest-trees and is at times very difficult. On the first day we reached the station Los Callejones, that is, "the place of the wood-roads," where we spent the night.

On the second day we proceeded as far as the Tres Champas, "the place of the three leaf huts," —*chican, chan* = little; *pa* = shelter; *champa* (*tšampa*) = little shelter, leaf huts. The huts of the montería, once established here and long since abandoned, have entirely disappeared; but an open hut still stands on the bank of the brook and affords some shelter to the traveller.

Soon after we had left Los Callejones and had ascended the hills, we saw a little lake on the right, far below us in a hollow, surrounded by walls of rock. The view of these cliffs, crowned by towering trees, with the water far below at their feet, is very impressive. This spot of natural beauty has no name, but in Mexico formations of this kind are called in general *hollos*, and I therefore called this particular spot *El Hollo.*

Some time later, about three leagues beyond Tres Champas, we found an obelisk set up to mark the boundary, bearing the name MEXICO on one side and GUATEMALA on the other, which will in future put an end to all doubts as to ownership in that part of the country. According to the latest disposition, therefore, Piedras Negras, which lies on the right bank of the Usumatsintla, belongs to Guatemala. The Mexican wood-cutting establishments still in this neighborhood will naturally all have to be removed.

On the third day we arrived safely at the site of the ruined city, the distance of which from Tenosique I estimated at about fifteen leagues.

The road from Tenosique to El Cayo runs by the ruined city and ends in a little open place, in which stands a great ceiba-tree. This place is bounded on the west side by rocky cliffs in which are several caves affording shelter to the wanderer. From this place, which I called *La Plazuela de las Cuevas*, a ravine, running transversely through the cliffs, leads to the Usumatsintla near by. On the heights to the right, and also below in the transverse valley, lay the huts of a wood-cutting establishment only recently abandoned and still in good condition. La Casa Principal, on an eminence near the river, was naturally the largest, and in it we comfortably established ourselves.

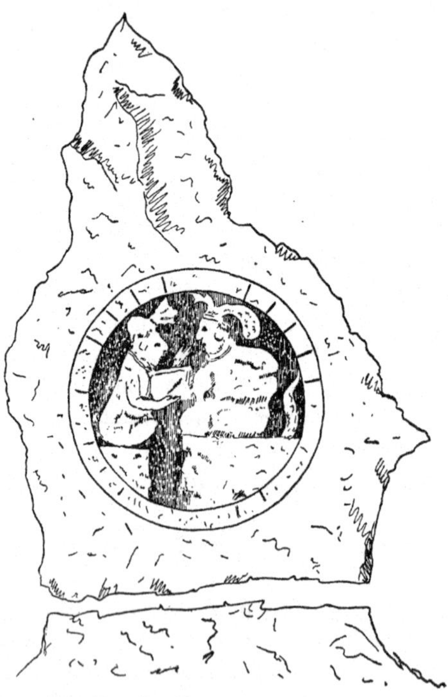

FIG. 15. — LA ROCA DE LOS SACRIFICIOS.

There, where the transverse valley opens towards the river, splendid sandbanks with blackish limestone rocks rising out of them invited us to bathe. The people of that region have named the place Piedras Negras after these rocks (Plate VII, 1).

One of these rocks, rising obliquely and pointed at the top, is especially noticeable, because there is carved upon its steeply inclined surface a circular design (Fig. 15) which resembles that upon the great sacrificial table (Fig. 19) on the esplanade before the temple of the eight stelæ. This fact seems to justify the surmise that on the rock in question were performed the sacrifices intended to appease the water deities; the blood of the victims trickling from the rock and mingling with the waters of the river. I called this rock *La Roca de los Sacrificios.*

Toward the end of the rainy season (October, November), however, the river rises at that point to the height of ten to fifteen metres, and all the sandbanks and rocks are entirely under water. Fortunately this was not the case when I encamped among the ruins. I was therefore able to take an excellent photograph of the place and to make a drawing of the sacrificial stone, whose design in low relief is very much worn away. Enough is left, however, to show two personages crouching opposite each other within a circle which is surrounded by a concentric band of glyphs. Only the spaces which contained the glyphs are still recognizable in outline; the glyphs themselves have quite disappeared. The diameter of the entire circular design is 166 cm.

From the sacrificial rock the ruined city extends two kilometres down stream (along the right bank). The transverse valley with its surrounding heights may be regarded as its southwestern, and the range of hills on which lies the upper city, or acropolis, as the northwestern boundary.

Some wood-cutters stated that in a direction up stream from the picture-rock there were more ruins, but I did not succeed in finding them. I thoroughly explored the chain of mountains above the rocks with the caves, but I found only remnants of terracing in the immediate vicinity of the caves. Therefore any other ruins could lie only between the mountain chain and the river.

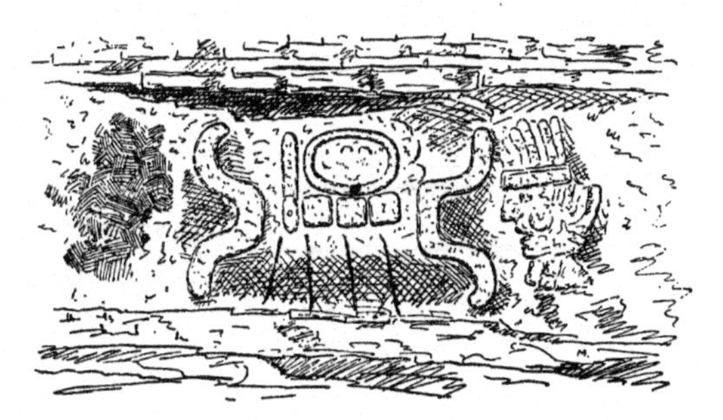

Fig. 16. — Sculpture upon Rock Wall.

Passing the caves and following the road to El Cayo for about half a kilometre, I turned to the left and discovered on a rock wall, about four metres above the level ground, a second piece of sculpture (Fig. 16), which was much worn. However I think I recognized a large hieroglyph in the middle, separated by an ornamental flourish on the right and on the left from two heads in profile. The head on the right (from the spectator) is still fairly well preserved; the one on the left has entirely scaled off. The height of the design is about one metre, the total length about two and a half metres.

We turned our attention chiefly to the acropolis, because the wood-cutters asserted that they had found large figures — *el rey, la reina* — in its vicinity.

The whole distance from the hills which slope down to the transverse valley as far as the acropolis is thickly strewn with the remains of old buildings which have succumbed to the weight of an overpowering vegetation.

Without stopping to examine these numerous heaps of ruins, we arrived at the lower steps of a monumental stairway on the southeastern slope of the acropolis. The stairway is ten metres wide and has only five steps, each one about 40 cm. in height. On either side of the stairway is an abutting vertical wall about five metres in length, faced with large stone slabs. At each wing these walls are continued by somewhat receding walls of common hewn blocks of smaller size, which form the retaining wall of the first terrace (Fig. 17).

From the platform of the stone stairway the second terrace is reached, whose right and left wings extend in the same manner as those of the first. But while the right wing of the terrace is quite empty, the *left wing* was formerly adorned with eight large stelæ, which now lie in confusion and for the most part broken in pieces upon the ground.

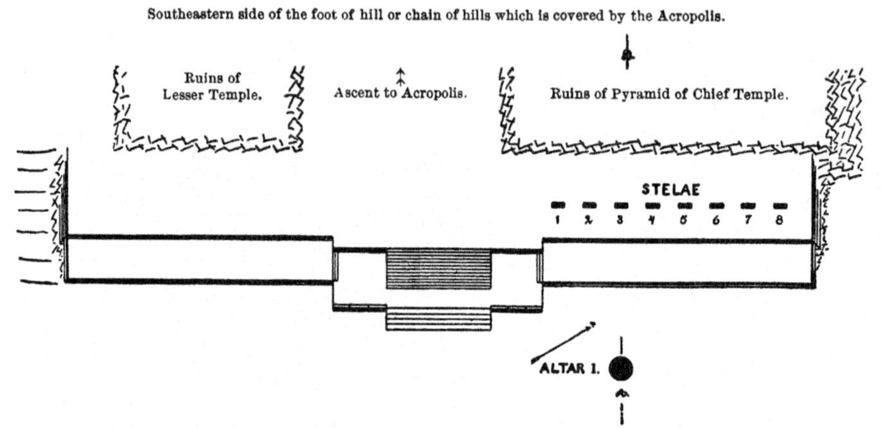

FIG. 17.— PIEDRAS NEGRAS: PLAN OF THE TERRACE OF THE EIGHT STELÆ.

In order to give a correct idea of the whole, I ought to state that on the right wing there must once have stood a lesser temple of inferior height, which is now wholly demolished, while on the left wing stood a large temple whose enormous pyramidal substructure with its numerous steps seems to form a part of the mountain against which it rests. Let me also add that the remaining terraces lead up to the acropolis by means of a saddle-shaped elevation between the two temple sites, in a line with the centre of the stone stairway, and that the upper terraces of the principal temple can be reached from the saddle by lateral ascents, not by centrally placed stairways, as is usually the case.

I searched the steps and the masses of ruins of the upper terraces to find out whether the lintels of the now ruined temple façade which had faced southeast, were ornamented with sculptures or not, for I had determined to dig them up if I could find the places where the entrances had been.

Unfortunately the confusion on the top platform was so great that it was impossible to determine which of the remnants of partially well-preserved masonry had belonged to the walls of the temple or had merely been part of the retaining walls of the steps of the pyramid. I was therefore unable to find the places where the entrances had been, but I concluded that the temple must have had a principal chamber in front and some smaller ones in the rear. I could not determine whether or not there had been chambers abutting against the main body of the whole structure ranged along the last terrace but one. Convinced that nothing short of an excavation on a very large scale would enable me to find the lintels, I was forced to confine myself to the clearing out of the eight stelæ on the second terrace from the bottom, and of the great round altar on the level ground in front of the temple.

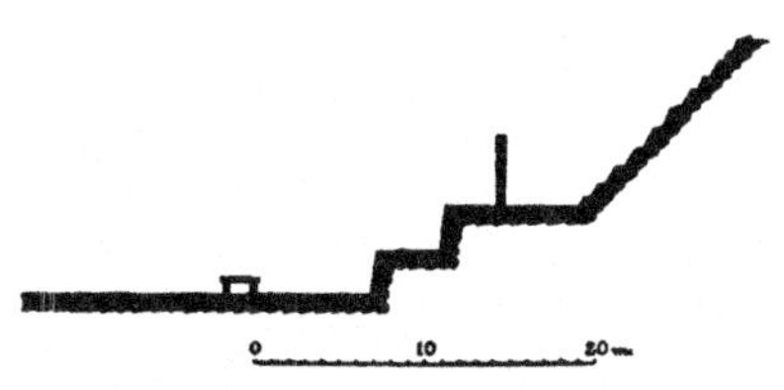

Fig. 18. — Piedras Negras: Terrace of the Eight Stelæ. Cross-section *a–b*.

Unfortunately this circular sacrificial table (No. 1) has been broken in two, probably by a falling tree, and the elaborate bas-relief on the upper surface is almost wholly destroyed by centuries of rain. It is now possible only to recognize two personages sitting opposite one another within the inner circle, surrounded by a concentric double band of glyphs (Fig. 19). The diameter of the circular stone slab is 213 cm. Its thickness is 35 cm., and the cylindrical outer edge is ornamented with a double row of glyphs. These glyphs, being less exposed to the action of the rain, are still in a tolerable state of preservation.

Fig. 19. — Design upon Upper Surface of Altar 1.

Three square pillars, each having ten glyphs on its front face, support the sacrificial stone. I photographed this circular altar after having had it cleaned (Plate VIII).

It took a whole week of hard work to prepare for photographing these stelæ, which probably marked the graves of persons of rank and also represented the principal divinities. Each stone was carefully excavated and set up on one of its narrow side faces by means of a windlass we had borrowed from a neighboring monteria, and then washed and brushed off in order to secure as good a picture as possible, after felling some trees which excluded the sunlight. Most of the stelæ had sculpture on the two broad faces and inscriptions on the narrow side faces. The face which had lain next to the ground was generally well preserved, while the upturned face was mostly destroyed.

Stela 1 (Plate XII). The whole height of this stone (now broken in two) is 425 cm., one metre of which was under ground. Its breadth is 136 cm.; thickness, 45 cm.

The sculpture on the front is wholly destroyed; that on the back, representing Ketsalkoatl, is very well preserved. Each narrow side face has a double row of glyphs, which have become quite indistinct.

The preserved relief represents the front view of a male figure, with an oval beardless face carved in very high relief. Upon the brow is placed the serpent's head, the upper row of teeth forming a diadem. Above the serpent's head is the turban, from the centre of which rises the ornamented feather-holder, and the plumes of feathers proceeding from it fall to the right and left. The god is clothed in a tunic reaching to his feet, ornamented with delicately incised Maltese crosses, and finished at the neck by a cape of scales. In his right hand the god holds feathers, and his left lies on the medallion of the cape.

The upper part of the relief consists of three horizontal rows of glyphs: $3 \times 7 = 21$. Along the edges a row of glyphs reached down to each shoulder: $8 + 10$, one glyph in each row being wholly destroyed, owing to the fracture of the stone, while all the rest are in an excellent state of preservation, — thirty-nine glyphs in all, two of which are destroyed. A small glyph also occurs at the base of the feather-holder.

Remnants of color were still visible, as follows: face, arms and garment, bright red; background, dark red; edge of garment, blue; breast-cape, blue; feathers, always green.

Stela 2 (Plate XV, 1). Broken in three pieces. Whole height of the fragments when joined together was 273 cm., of which 63 cm. were sunk in the ground, and 195 cm. were covered with sculpture. Width, 68 cm.; thickness, 43–45 cm.

The figure, probably of a god, on one of the broad faces, is wholly destroyed; that, presumably of a man, on the other is pretty well preserved. One of the narrow side faces has an upright figure in bas-relief, and the other has an inscription in two perpendicular rows. The side faces have both become quite indistinct. Though the well-preserved figure presents very nearly a front view, the face, now crumbled away, is quite in profile. In his right hand the personage represented holds a kind of chain, in his left an ornamental pouch. On the right shoulder there is a grotesque face, and at the girdle, from which depend broad sash-ends, there is a mask of unusual size with eyes turned inward of a Mongolian type. The helmet is formed of an animal with the face turned upward. From its breast proceeds the feather-holder, terminating in a plume of feathers above; while feathers also fall toward the back, and a fantastic little creature, something like a bird, preceded by a much smaller, indefinable one, is represented as creeping upward on the feather-holder. The only traces of color still visible are bits of red on the background.

Stela 3 (Plate XIII). Broken in three pieces. Whole height 410 cm., of which one metre had been sunk into the ground. Width, 135–140 cm.; thickness, about 42 cm.

The two narrow side faces have double rows of inscriptions imperfectly preserved. This stela lay sunk in the ground in a horizontal position, with the sculptured side, which had formerly faced the esplanade, turned skyward, and though it was covered with foliage and earth, it was so badly crumbled that all the finer detail had disappeared. Only the main outlines of the figure were still discernible, and these I copied before I had the stone turned over.

The personage on the weather-beaten side of the stela presents an entire front view (Fig. 20). He seems to hold his right arm against his breast and the left arm against his side. The head is surmounted by a tall turban-like head-dress, to the outside of which is attached a plume of feathers, while another plume still higher up proceeds from an ornament on the top of the turban.

Fig. 20. — Sketch of the Weather-beaten Side of Stela 3.

It can no longer be determined whether this figure, following the rule of the stelæ of Yāxchilan, represents a human being of rank, or even, by way of exception, a god. On the other hand it may safely be asserted that the principal figure on the side which had formerly faced the temple and had afterward fallen face downward, represented Ketsalkoatl in the character of a beneficent god.

The sculpture on this side, which had lain upon the earth, was admirably preserved (Plate XIII). The principal figure is represented dressed and adorned like the representation of a god on Stela 1, but enthroned, sitting Turkish fashion, on a bench. The fronts of the two pillars supporting the throne are ornamented with large glyphs, resembling each other, while the front face of the bench, the whole length of which is elaborately ornamented with scroll-work, exhibits the small figure of a man.

The god sits cross-legged on the throne, clad in the usual tunic ornamented with little crosses, but instead of the cape of scales he wears a simple necklace. The face is executed in alto-relief, and directly upon the forehead (without the intervening serpent's head) is placed the great ribbed turban. The holder with the plume of feathers is here also attached to the side of the turban, but this time in a horizontal position to leave room for the large, perfectly preserved inscription, which occupies the whole upper part of the stela.

On the right hand of the god is what might be called "the box of felicities," — a pendant to "the chest of good-fortune" and "the rope of honey" in the representations of like significance on the deity-side of the stelæ of Yāxchilan! The box is of East-Asiatic shape, and ornamented with the so-called four-leaved clover. I think the stopper, which has become indistinct, is meant to represent the head of a bee.

On the left of the god sits a man who looks expectantly up at him.

Seven horizontal rows of six glyphs each fill out the upper portion of the stela, and groups of three hang down on each side of the head, — forty-eight glyphs in all, plus the two on the pillars supporting the bench.

The remains of color are bright red on the face, arm, and garment; dark red in the background; blue and green on the ornamentation, and the feathers green, as always.

Stela 4 (Plate XIV). Probably broken in three pieces. The height of the two pieces covered with sculpture was estimated at 305 cm., to which must be added at least one metre for the lowest unornamented piece. Width, 135 cm.; thickness, about 40 cm.

Two rows of glyphs are still discernible on the narrow side faces. The sculpture on what is presumably the deity-side is wholly effaced; that of the other side is preserved, excepting the face of the principal figure, across which the fracture runs.

The sculpture represents the front view of a richly dressed person of rank, with the now shattered face in profile. The gigantic, strangely intertwined head-dress is especially noticeable. On the ground to the right and to the left of the principal figure sits a prisoner. The rope with which the arms are bound can be distinctly seen.

Remains of red are still visible only in the background and on the uncovered parts of the body. All the other colors have disappeared.

Stela 5 (Plate XV, 2). The lowermost portion of this stela, very little of which can have been covered by sculpture, lies all in pieces under the roots of a giant tree. The preserved fragment is 255 cm. in height, 123 cm. in breadth, and about 40 cm. thick.

An inscription in two vertical rows is still discernible on each of the narrow side faces. The low relief on one of the broad faces is unfortunately wholly effaced, but the wavy lines still to be seen on the surface indicate that it must once have been divided into several compartments filled in with small figures. The carefully executed sculpture of the other broad face is in a good state of preservation, and shows an entirely different arrangement from that of the other stelæ.

The principal figure carved in profile sits in what might be called European fashion, upon a stone bench covered with a tiger skin (the head of the tiger is plainly recognizable). The face of the principal figure and a part of the helmet have unfortunately scaled off. Both hands hold a sceptre with a grotesque face.

In front of the principal figure, but a little lower down, stands a second personage with a tiara on his head. Extending along the whole length of the back of the sitting figure is a rod ornamented to resemble a snake-skin, which gradually assumes the form of a snake and curves down over the two personages. From a mask on the ground, a variety of scroll-work twines upward in the narrow space behind the rod. Upon this scroll-work rise, one above the other, two emaciated and apparently dying forms, while a third form with an extremely expressive countenance bends down over the curves of the serpent toward the helmet ornaments of the sitting figure. Above the curve described by the serpent, resting on a base of scroll-work, is a large bird with a delicately executed human head. This bird is not unlike those which surmount the cruciform bas-reliefs in the sanctuaries of the two Temples of the Cross at Palenque. There are three glyphs above the head of the personage with the tiara.

The exposed portions of the bodies of the two personages show remnants of bright red, the tiger's eyes are bright red, the background is dark red, and the ornamental scroll-work shows traces of blue and green.

Stela 6 (Plate XV, 3). Whole height of the stone, 293 cm., 228 cm. of which are covered by the sculpture. Width at the bottom, 75 cm., and at the top, 85 cm. Thickness, about 40–43 cm.

One of the narrow side faces has an upright figure in bas-relief; the other has two perpendicular rows of glyphs. On one of its broad faces the stela had a bas-relief, now quite crumbled away, and on the other the figure of a god sitting in a niche in half or almost high relief.

While the niche with the deity is cut very deep into the stone, the surrounding glyphs and ornamentations are in very low relief. Owing to these contrasts, it is difficult to obtain a satisfactory photograph of the whole.

The god supports his right hand at his girdle, and holds in his left an ornamental pouch, which hangs far down over the edge of the niche. He wears a breast-cape of scales and the familiar horizontal breastplate. His head is surmounted by a serpent's head. Over this is a small human head, and over the latter the closed hand out of which proceeds the feather-holder with the feathers.

There is ornamental work on the surfaces above and below the niche, and a perpendicular row of glyphs of about twenty little characters runs along the right and the left edge of the stone. Most of the glyphs are well preserved, but some have become indistinct and others have been broken off. In addition to these there are some very delicately incised miniature inscriptions: 3 + 4 + 3 at the very bottom; 3 + 4 on both sides of the feather-holder, and 3 + 3 still higher up.

Remnants of color: face, arms, body, and thighs of the deity, bright red; serpent's head, hands, and feather-holder, likewise red; breast-cape, green, and all the feathers, green.

Stela 7 (Plate XVI). The stone is broken off obliquely across the neck of the principal figure. Whole height (length), 349 cm., of which 277 cm. are covered with sculpture; breadth, 98 cm.; and thickness, 47–50 cm.

The two narrow side faces have an inscription in double rows.

The sculpture on one of the broad faces, which was in very low relief, is entirely destroyed. That of the other, which had fallen face downward and of which the principal figure is in very high relief, is in an excellent state of preservation, even, partially, as to color.

A warrior of high rank, represented in front view, holds a lance with a fantastic face in his right hand, a shield and an ornamental pouch on his left arm; his tunic, falling to the knee, has elaborate feather-work in front and a border of sea-shells. The girdle is almost quite covered up, and from it fall sash-ends which appear below the feather garment and exhibit an elaborate pattern of Maya embroidery. The ankles and knees are encircled by ornamental bands.

The head-dress can best be described as follows: upon the forehead rests a flat omega ⁀∩⁀ ornamented with little discs, which is surmounted by a high omega Ω. The latter must be regarded as the jaws of a serpent which hold a human head, the row of teeth on the upper jaw forming a little penthouse for it. From the two extremities of the flat omega, framing face, neck, and breast, and likewise ornamented with discs, depends a U-shaped band, from the middle of which a bow with ends falls to the girdle in the form of an inverted tau ⊥. At the point where the bow appears there is a little death's-head in a horizontal position. To the top of the high omega are attached two volutes, out of which proceed two feather-holders with plumes of feathers falling right and left. Above the volutes rises a kind of architectural crest surrounded by three great, broad feathers of the wild turkey (*Meleagris ocelata*) and feather scroll-work.

To the right of the warrior chieftain a captive kneels on the ground with his arms bound together, holding his toothed sword, point downward, in his right hand. The distinguishing mark of a captive, in the form of two little glyphs, is carved upon the sword.

The remnants of color are bright red on the face and other portions of the body of the principal figure, also in the vacant space enclosed by the high omega (serpent's mouth); all the disc chains of the ornaments, shaped thus Ω, U, ⊥, C, are sky-blue (this color is of especially fine quality, and so distinct that it admits of no error); all the feather-work is green; the naked portions of the captive's body are bright red.

Stela 8 (Plate XVII). This stela is broken into several pieces. I was able to fit together the separately taken negatives of the three largest pieces, which are covered by the most important part of the sculpture. The lowermost fragment is still sunk deep in the soil of the terrace, in a perpendicular position; it displays, however, only a very little carving.

The breadth of this stone is 128 cm.; thickness, 43 cm. Its former height may have been something over four metres in all.

The two narrow side faces were decorated with double rows of glyphs. One of the broad faces, as it seemed to me, had once been covered by only an inferior kind of sculpture, which is now quite destroyed with the exception of a few slight remains. The more favored broad face has for its principal figure a warrior of high rank. This figure is represented in full front view, and his dress and head-dress exhibit extremely elaborate detail. His richly ornamented short upper garment has a border of sea-shells, and the loin-cloth below it is a network of cords. In his right hand the warrior holds a lance tipped with a little image; in his left he holds a shield; his head-dress is an enormous structure of scroll- and feather-work, and the top of the stela is finished off by three horizontal rows of glyphs of, I believe, twelve characters each. From each end of the lowest row four additional glyphs extend downward. Below the base line of the principal figure there are two rows of glyphs of eight characters each, which do not, however, occupy the entire breadth of the stone, because the captives kneeling to the right and to the left extend a little below the base line. It is plainly discernible that both the captives have their arms bound.

Remnants of color: the skin of all the figures is bright red; background, dark red; ornamentation, partly red, partly green, and partly blue; feather ornaments, green.

The eight sepulchral stelæ are all of a yellowish white limestone, hard enough in the dry season, but somewhat soft in the rainy season, when they are soaked with water; and it is this that hastens the destruction of the sculptured stones. Generally speaking, the sculpture is well and clearly executed on all the stones, with a great wealth of detail. There was no trace of yellow, black, or white among the remnants of color, either because these colors cannot withstand the action of the elements or because they were never used.

The stelæ having all been successfully photographed, we applied ourselves to the task of thoroughly exploring the acropolis, the principal structure of which is undoubtedly the temple of the eight stelæ. Following the ascents belonging to the continuation of the stone stairway (Fig. 17), we reached the plateaus of the mountain chain, which had everywhere been levelled and prepared for the building of numerous edifices of stone.

We examined the numerous half-ruined structures, — remains of chambers, passages, rear-chambers with triangularly arched vaults, half-buried entrances, etc., — but in all that débris we found no sculptured stones. Our attention was especially attracted by a very long edifice which we called *La Casa Grande.* It consists of a long, now ruined vestibule, with an entrance in its medial wall to a rear apartment of equal length, whose vaulted ceiling has fallen, while the long back wall still stands intact. Though the mountain range descends to the river in very steep and often perpendicular cliffs, I nevertheless succeeded in climbing down between the rocks with one of my men, in order to make a tour of inspection through that part of the city which lies nearest to the river. But here also, among countless heaps of ruins, we found nothing worth noting.

Between the acropolis and the hills of the transverse valley, where the cabins of the wood-cutters lie, the otherwise rolling country forms an extensive level area which occupies about the middle of the city. Here we found two large, square sacrificial altars, to which I afterward gave the numbers 3 and 4. It is clear that these altars, which I cleaned and photographed, must have had reference to some temples near by, in particular to a large temple which I afterward called *El Templo de la Estela de las Víctimas.*

At the foot of the dilapidated pyramid of this important edifice, along its south-southwestern side, we found four gigantic stelæ, lying flat on the ground, which I afterward numbered 16, 17, 18, 19. The stelæ had all fallen with the important sculptured faces upward, which were consequently wholly destroyed. We comforted ourselves with the hope that the faces sunk in the earth would have well-preserved sculptures. But this hope was not fulfilled. Some had no sculpture at all on the buried faces, and others displayed only certain wavy lines. The stones had evidently not been able to withstand the moisture of the earth; nevertheless double rows of glyphs could still be recognized on the narrow side faces of all the four stelæ, one even showing a figure in profile.

Somewhat discouraged by the negative results of our investigations of the four giant stelæ, we explored the forest in an easterly direction from the Temple of the Sacrificial Stela, and came to a small half-ruined structure, the ground-plan of which may be thus described: The projecting right wing, and also the now ruined left wing, had each four connected narrow chambers surrounding a middle room located somewhat below their plane in such a manner that the fourth narrow chamber ran the whole length of the building and was therefore common to both the wings (Fig. 21). A now ruined entrance in the south front led into the middle chamber, which had a large stone bench built into it. The monteros, whose imagination is always stirred up by the thought of *casas cerradas*, not perceiving the entrance obstructed by débris, had made a breach in the wall of the narrow right side, but do not seem to have found the hoped-for treasure.

As I was not prepared to undertake further excavations likely to consume much additional time, after a stay of fifteen days among the ruins,

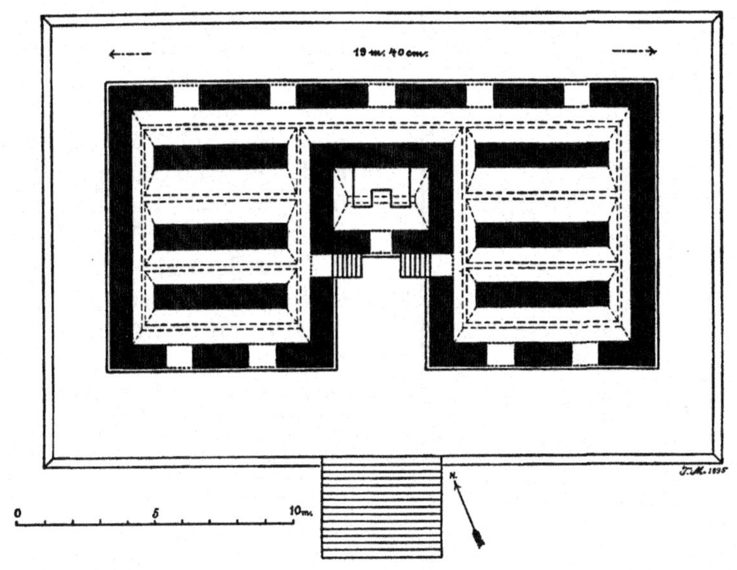

Fig. 21. — Piedras Negras: Plan of the Temple of the Eight Chambers.

I concluded to set out with my men on my way back to Tenosique, whence I returned to Yucatan.

In 1897, while on my expedition to Yāxchilan, I again passed through Piedras Negras, but without attempting excavations of any kind.

Not until the year 1899, when I had organized an expedition under the auspices of the Peabody Museum of Cambridge, Mass., for the further exploration of the ruined cities on the Usumatsintla and of the Indian territories lying in that region, did I find it expedient to subject Piedras Negras to another investigation, in order to obtain definite results for the Museum, before risking time and money in uncertain wanderings, especially since the perpetually discontented men from Tenosique are never to be counted on for any length of time.

In the forests lying along the banks of the river, new lumber camps had been established since my last visit, which, by their offer of large sums of money, had attracted all the available men for miles around, so that I found great difficulty in securing a few men for my expedition. By the end of August, however, I was able to leave Tenosique with three men and the necessary pack-animals, having already sent a store of provisions and other things to El Cayo.

The palmleaf huts of the montería of Piedras Negras had entirely disappeared, and everything was already quite overgrown by the luxuriant tropical vegetation. For this reason I had to find quarters for myself and my men in one of the caves near the place of the ceiba. These caves afforded us excellent shelter in the rainy season, which was now in progress. We supplied our animals with fodder by daily cutting branches from the ramon-tree, which fortunately abounds in these forests.

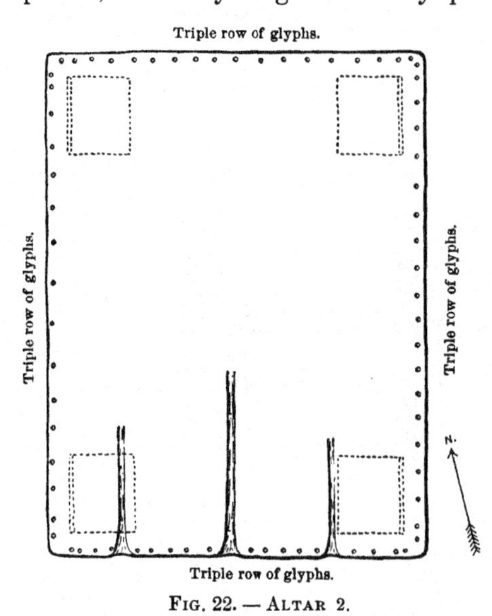

Fig. 22. — Altar 2.

We devoted the months of September, October, and November (1899) to the further exploration of the ruined city, with such good results this time that Piedras Negras now ranks with Palenque and Yāxchilan in respect of the number and importance of its sculptures.

I will now proceed to describe the new discoveries consecutively, in connection with those previously made by me, in order to be perfectly clear.

The Temple of the Three Stelæ 9, 10, 11, forming a part of the acropolis. Leaving the stone stairway of five steps and passing along the foot of the acropolis mountain range in the direction of the river, we came upon a well-preserved, rectangular sacrificial table or altar resting upon four pillars, which I called No. 2 (Fig. 22).

The length of the table is 220 cm.; breadth, 172 cm.; thickness, 35 cm.

Certain wavy lines on the surface of the table seem to indicate that it must once have had a sculptured bas-relief upon it, which is now totally worn away. The grooves for carrying off the blood, sloping toward one of the edges, are still plainly visible.

Around the four narrow faces of the table run three parallel rows of glyphs, which are quite small and have nearly all become indistinct. The four edges of the table have been pierced by a series of little holes at an angle of 45°. Could they have served for suspending the skulls of the victims?

On the faces corresponding to the long sides of the table, the four supporting pillars have three perpendicular rows of glyphs of three characters each, that is, $4 \times 9 = 36$ glyphs, which are very well preserved, protected, as they have been, by the sacrificial stone.

The monteros, who perpetrate a great deal of mischief among the ruins of this wilderness, in spite of all prohibitions on the part of the Mexican government, have torn out one of the supporting pillars of the table, suspecting hidden treasures beneath it. It was, therefore, an easy matter to put the detached pillar in a good light and photograph its inscription (Plate X). The other three inscriptions, owing to the projecting edges of the sacrificial stone, are in an unfavorable light, and it would be necessary to make a mould of them if they are to be reproduced. The height of the little pillars is 91 cm., about one-third of which was sunk into the ground.

A little way back of the sacrificial table rise the steps and terraces belonging to a small temple standing on a considerable eminence, the front apartment of which is in ruins, while remains of the rear apartment are still standing, — a fact which I had already observed during my first expedition. Among the débris of the ruined façade I found the various pieces of the lintel slab, which I called No. 5. Unfortunately its bas-relief was almost wholly effaced. It was, however, still possible to discern that it resembled a scene similar to that on lintel No. 4 (Plate XXXII), that is, warriors kneeling before a *Halachvinic* (warrior chieftain), with descriptive glyphs overhead. It was possible to recognize distinctly that the chieftain, who holds a lance in his right hand, has on the same peculiar round head-dress as the one worn by the principal person in the bas-relief of lintel 4. Unfortunately the whole thing was broken into such small pieces and was so weather-worn that it was impossible to fit the fragments together so that they could be photographed.

Upon the second terrace, rising about eight metres above the natural level of the ground, formerly stood the three stelæ which, in my enumeration of the whole, I have numbered 9, 10, 11. They are all three broken in pieces, but most of them having fallen with the sculptured face downward, they are in that respect well preserved. The backs of the stelæ were smooth, the sculptured fronts had faced the esplanade, and the sides had also been ornamented with sculpture.

Stela 9 (Plate XVIII, 1). Of this stela three fragments, which held the most important part of the sculpture, lay on the ground, while the bottom piece and a piece of one of the upper corners could not be found. The stone may have been about four metres in height; the breadth is 112 cm.;

the thickness, 42 cm. The two narrow side faces have a double row of little glyphs, most of which have become quite indistinct. One of the broad faces is smooth, without any sculpture whatever; the other has a bas-relief, of which the principal figure is a richly dressed warrior chieftain in front view, whose right hand holds a foreshortened lance surmounted by a death-mask, and his left arm a shield and ornamented pouch. The short tunic has a fringe of sea-shells, and over it, beginning at the neck, falls a long scarf which also seems to be ornamented with shells. (A similar scarf with shells, of a somewhat different design, is worn by several figures of warriors at Yāxchilan.)

Above the forehead on a flat omega ⌒ of little discs, lies the main body of the circular head-dress, with a small glyph in the centre. To either side of the sphere is attached an ornament, worked in elaborate detail, from which proceed spreading plumes of feathers, while on top there is an expressive mask, which is evidently meant to look like a face, whether regarded in its normal position or upside down. Above this face great bundles of feathers proceed out of the top and sides of an architectural ornament, thus giving this remarkable head-dress the form of a cross. A prisoner of war, with his arms bound, kneels on the ground to the right of the warrior.

Although the sculpture has now largely crumbled away, it still shows traces of very nice detail in execution. There are no remnants of color visible.

Stela 10 (Plate XIX). This stela was no doubt thrown down by a falling tree upon the ground in front of the pyramid, and broken in two pieces in its fall. The lower half with the corresponding portion of sculpture fell face downward, and is consequently preserved, while the upper half with the upper half of the sculpture is destroyed, because it fell face upward, owing, no doubt, to a rotary motion in falling.

The height of the lower piece, taking a perpendicular line through the centre, measured 230 cm., the upper piece 185 cm.; total height, therefore, 415 cm. Breadth toward the centre, 108 cm.; thickness, 38 cm.

The back is smooth. One of the narrow side faces has two rows of handsome glyphs, and an initial glyph which occupies a space equal to that of four other glyphs. These glyphs have crumbled away on the lower piece, but on the upper one, which was buried deep in the earth, they are well preserved, making 1 + 14 preserved glyphs. The other narrow side face has an upright figure in profile, and above it eight glyphs which have become rather indistinct. Of this sculpture the breast, face, head-dress, and the eight glyphs belong to the upper piece.

The broad face with the preserved piece of sculpture has at the bottom (not counting, of course, the portion sunk in the ground) two horizontal rows of large glyphs, four in each row, that is, eight in all. These are executed in very flat relief, while the principal figure is in very high relief, and they are not in the style of writing usual on monuments, but are a simplified form of it, which I call "the second manner of Maya writing."

Above the glyphs stands a gigantic figure in profile representing "the man with the tiger's paws," well preserved, from the tiger's paw to the girdle. He wears closely fitting leggings of tiger-skin, and his foot has tiger's claws.

In front of this figure is a kind of throne embellished by a splendid head and a certain kind of ornamentation in horizontal lines. Upon this throne sits, in Turkish fashion, a personage of rank drawn in profile, with his back turned to the principal figure, and well preserved as far as the forehead.

As to remains of color, traces of red can still be discerned on the arms and thighs of the person of rank and also on the throne.

It is to be regretted that the upper part of this stela is destroyed, for it would be interesting to compare "the man with the tiger's claws" of Piedras Negras with the one at Seibal.

Stela 11 (Plate XX, 1). I found a stela with a god, which had fallen from the edge of the second terrace and was broken in two pieces. It lay inclining toward the lowest terrace at an angle of 45°. It was quite impossible to set up the heavy stones in this desperately awkward position. I, therefore, had them hauled down on logs to the first terrace, where they were turned over and photographed.

Whole height of the stone, 395 cm.; breadth in the middle (owing to the convexity of the side faces), 3 + 103 + 3 cm.; thickness, 45 cm.

The back of the stela is perfectly plain; the narrow side faces, however, are covered with sculpture. On one of the narrow sides there is a well-drawn figure in profile with three little glyphs by the side of its plume of feathers; above the latter a double row of glyphs, 5 + 5, and quite at the top, but weather-worn, the initial hieroglyph, which occupies a space equalling that of two other glyphs, amounting to fourteen glyphs in all. This side face is very well preserved.

The other side face has a figure in profile standing upright; behind it and crowded closely up against it, is another figure, a head shorter. The space above these figures is filled in by a double row of glyphs: 7 + 7 = 14. The sculptured figures on this face, though recognizable, are not so clear and well preserved as those on the other.

The lowest portion of the broad sculptured side is naturally smooth. It measures 108 cm., of which two-thirds had been walled into the ground. Then follows 101 cm. of decoration in very flat relief, reaching to the lower edge of the niche. In the middle of this bas-relief and on its base line is a kind of circular altar over which a tiger-skin is spread, with some pieces of wood laid crosswise. Upon this lies a naked human form, whose head, arms, and thighs hang down over the altar. From the opened abdomen of the victim (?) rises a bulbous vessel, out of the neck of which comes an erect plume of feathers. In the background rises a T-shaped structure of beams, from either arm of which depends a graceful arabesque of grotesque faces and scroll-work. All traces of color have vanished from the lower part of this relief, while on the sculpture in the niche, which lay concavely over the ground but untouched by it, the colors have been preserved quite distinct and fresh. Only the very top of the stela, which was buried in the earth, is very much disintegrated.

The god, probably Ketsalkoatl, sits cross-legged in Asiatic fashion, on a step in the niche. He is represented in full face, almost wholly in high relief. His right hand rests on his right thigh, and he holds an ornamental pouch in his left hand. A horizontal breastplate with a little mask upon it is attached to the green breast-cape. The cuffs at his wrists are green, likewise the round ear-pegs. All the naked parts of the body — the face, arms, and thighs — are bright red.

The head of the figure is surmounted by a green serpent's head with red eyes and red open jaws, out of which develops the great ribbed turban, surmounted in its turn by an expressive little head. The scroll-work to the right and left of the serpent's head is partly red and partly green. All the feather-work is bluish-green; the rest of the background is dark red.

The niche is finished at the top by a curtain, looped up in four places, and fastened to the edge above by tying, while along each side of the niche runs a wide border of four and a half simple glyphs (in the second manner of writing).

A horizontal line above the curtain separates the latter from the ornamentation at the top, which seems to have consisted of grotesque faces and scroll-work, but is now very much worn by the action of the elements.

The Temple of the Lintel with the Consecration of the Warriors and of the Stela with the God and the Victims on the Platform Above. In Spanish simply: *El Templo de la Estela de las Víctimas.* During my second exploration of Piedras Negras I devoted especial attention to the temple at the foot of the pyramid, of which I had found the four great stelæ lying upon the ground, and the two great sacrificial altars, because I was convinced that the site ought to yield much more. I climbed up by the half-ruined steps of the pyramid, for there was no trace of a front stairway, and investigated the ruins on the platform above.

For the better comprehension of the plan of the entire structure, let me say that the façade of the temple in question fronts south-south-west. On this side the pyramid steps with their retaining walls formed the connection between the normal ground level and the highest platform, which merges in the mountain range behind, upon whose receding summits no further vestiges of buildings could be found.

The ruined temple itself is an oblong structure of the size usual for a building, with a front apartment of three entrances, after the manner of building in these parts. The façade is in ruins, but the entire rear wall as well as the side walls are still standing. A stairway, built against the middle of the rear wall of the temple, once led up to the flat roof, which is now fallen in.

It is possible that the temple had chambers in the rear, corresponding to the long vestibule, but this could not be ascertained without undertaking an excavation. It would be still more difficult to determine whether the edifice had a roof-comb or not.

Convinced that the façade must have had three entrances, I made a slight excavation on the platform near the middle of the mass of ruins in front of the temple and was fortunate enough, after removing a few stones, to find the sought-for middle lintel, which was adorned on its lower face with a well-executed, very interesting piece of sculpture. The slab was cracked in two, but, excepting the line of fracture, the sculpture is admirably preserved, only the colors have entirely disappeared. I called this lintel No. 2 (Plate XXXI).

Length of slab, 129 cm.	Length of sculpture, 113 cm.
Breadth of slab, 58 cm.	Breadth of sculpture, 49½ cm.
Thickness of slab, 15 cm.	

Upon the base-line of the picture stands the principal figure, the Halachvinic (halatšvinik), or warrior chieftain, richly dressed and wearing a great helmet with plumes of feathers. In his outstretched right hand he holds a lance, on his left arm a quadrangular shield. Behind him stands the second in command, or adjutant, likewise armed with lance and shield. To the point of the lance are attached five little hieroglyphs, probably expressing the command which the Halachvinic is giving the six warriors kneeling before him. These warriors, doubtless subordinate chieftains, are all well dressed, and wear on their heads helmets with plumes of feathers. Each holds a lance in his right hand; the shield on the left arm being concealed, owing to the position of the body. The sculpture is bordered on the left (from the spectator) by six large hieroglyphs, — one large initial glyph and five chronological representations of faces; on the right by two perpendicular rows of small glyphs, 10 + 10; on top by two horizontal rows of small glyphs, 22 + 22. In addition to these are thirty-six still smaller glyphs, in three rows of twelve each directly over the kneeling warriors. It seems evident that six of these glyphs, in two columns of three each, belong to each of the warriors. In all, six large glyphs and one hundred and five smaller ones.

After so successfully finding lintel No. 2, we at once proceeded to search for No. 1. But this time the matter was not so easy. As the esplanade in front of the temple is scarcely three metres wide, the débris of the ruined façade had mingled with that of the retaining walls of the terraces, and, to add to the confusion, a gigantic tree, blown down by a storm, lay at full length along the dilapidated slope from the former entrance of the temple to the foot of the substructure. As we were in the midst of the rainy season, it was impossible to burn the half-decayed, water-logged trunk. Hindered by the tree, we searched about to the best of our ability. At last below, on the ground at the base of the pyramid, we found a small corner-piece of sculpture, which I at once recognized as belonging to the sought-for lintel; and this strengthened my conviction that the main portion, covered by débris, must lie somewhere under the tree.

This corner-piece (Plate XXX) justifies the surmise that lintel No. 1 is also of great interest. It represents a scene quite different from that of No. 2, and is possibly taken from every-day life. It may be assumed that this piece of sculpture was of two kinds: A border of figures and glyphs in very flat relief, and a group of small, very delicately executed figures in half relief, occupying the central portion of the face of the slab. The fragment of border on this corner-piece shows the small figure of a man dressed in a long tunic held together over the abdomen by a broad girdle, to the front of which is attached a large face-mask. His head is covered by a simple cap, and his hands seem to be bound together in front of his neck. Five miniature glyphs are incised in front of the little man and on either side, above his head, the lowest glyph of a short series is seen. The little half-relief figure of the middle picture is that of a man with arms crossed over his breast and his face entirely demolished.

Stela 12 (Plate XXI). We were quite unsuccessful in finding lintel No. 3, owing to the uncertainty as to whether it lay buried under débris above on the esplanade, or somewhere on one of the terraces, or below on the level ground. In its stead we found in a little open square on the same platform, at the left flank of the temple, the shattered remains of a great stela (the twelfth in my general enumeration) with a god the sculpture of which, in spite of the fractures, was very well preserved, as all the pieces had fallen with the sculptured face downward. After we had disengaged the three lower pieces and set them up, we came to the conclusion that the entire upper half was missing. We therefore examined the ruined slope on the side on which we had found the stela, and finally, far below on a terrace about three metres above the level ground, we found the missing piece, which we also excavated and set up.

Under such difficulties we took some negatives on celluloid plates, which we afterwards carefully cut out and fitted together on a glass plate, thus procuring a picture 47½ cm. in length, which distinctly shows all the sculpture still preserved.

I estimate the height of the sculpture from the base line at the bottom upon which the lowest row of captives are crouching, to the very top, at about three metres, to which at least one metre more should be added for the lowest undecorated part. The breadth of the stone is 103 cm., and the thickness 42 cm.

The back of the stela has no sculpture at all, but the narrow side faces have double rows of glyphs, partly preserved and partly destroyed.

The god occupying the upper part of the stela sits upon a kind of throne, with the right leg hanging down over it, and the left one drawn up and lying upon it. In his right hand he holds a kind of lance, and his left hand rests upon his left knee. He wears a carefully executed cape of scales or short feathers, and a necklace of small leaf-shaped plates (not round beads), and upon his breast a handsome cruciform medallion, which consists of a little bright-red figure holding a St. Andrew's cross with both hands and standing on a triple pendant, while to the right and left of his shoulders a similar triple ornament completes the form of a cross. His helmet supports a great bird's head, from the fan-like crest of which great curved plumes proceed. The graceful figure of the god, painted bright red, inclines graciously toward the priests, who are below him and are bringing him a number of captives for sacrifice. One of the priests wears as a head-dress a tiger's head with red claws and bunches of feathers (?) coming out of the mouth; the other wears a peculiar pointed hat with a large round cushion on top, from which two long feathers stand up.

On the lowest base line I count six captives, bound together with ropes. Among them is an old man, with emaciated limbs, sadly casting his eyes on the ground. Perhaps his arts of magic have brought him to this distressing pass. He holds a little plaited box in his left hand. Close beside him is an ugly "savage" of that period. His face is hairy, and he looks like a real barbarian. Another captive holds up six slender little sticks.

In the middle, above this lowest group, there are two more figures, while two priests stand upon steps to the right and left. Upon a still higher step sits a man somewhat more adorned, perhaps a captive of high rank.

There are twelve personages in all represented upon this stela. The custom of filing the teeth in the shape of a saw seems to have prevailed among these condemned men, as can be seen through the half-open lips. Almost all of them have a number of knobs or beads around the lobe of the ear, and also on the chin or on top of the nose. All the captives have miniature hieroglyphs incised upon the breast or thigh or on the background in their immediate vicinity. There are likewise several delicately executed inscriptions on the throne. I find in all 2 + 2 + 2 + 2 + 3 + 3 + 4 + 2 + 3 + 3 + 2 + 3 + 3 + 4 + 4 + 4 + 4 + 3, making a total of 53 hieroglyphs, of which number only the three beside the handsome tassel have become indistinct.

Various remains of bright-red color are still to be seen on the naked portions of the body of the principal personages, as also on some of the ornaments, the inscriptions, and on the background generally. All other colors have disappeared.

Stela 13 (Plate XVIII, 2). Upon the ground below I found a stela of medium size, broken in three pieces, which had probably fallen down from the highest terrace. To this one I gave the number 13.

The whole height of the stela may once have been very nearly three metres. Height of sculpture from the base line to the top, 170 cm.; breadth about 95 cm., and thickness 36 cm.

The narrow side faces have a double row of glyphs, very much impaired. The back of the stela is plain.

The broad sculptured face shows a richly dressed personage who is scattering cocoa-beans (?), the symbol of prosperity (?), with his right hand, and holding with his left an ornamental pouch with an appendage of conventionalized rattles. The little glyph on the front of the pouch shows the number 13 = ⁞ ‖ = *oxlahun* — on one side of an oval containing a little bust: equivalent to *ahau-Kabtun*. It is probable that the meaning of this glyph is *oxlahun-ahau-Kabtun*,* that is, the thirteenth series of years.

This presumably beneficent deity wears buskins and breeches of tiger-skin, a red girdle with a red border of sea-shells, and a very handsome face-mask in front, from which depends a long bow with ends.

The breast-cape consists of little cylinders and stone beads. Below the cape the breast is further adorned with a medallion, upon the smooth surface of which I am unable to discover a design. The helmet is ornamented in front with the head of an animal and on top and at the back with plumes of feathers. The clear spaces of the background display delicately incised glyphs, 3 + 4 + 4. Traces of red are discernible only on the pouch, the face, and the girdle. All other colors have disappeared.

Stela 14 (Plate XX, 2). Buried deep under a mass of débris at the foot of the half-pyramid, I found a stela with a niche resembling No. 6, but of better workmanship. This also had doubtless fallen from the top terrace, and in its fall had been broken in two pieces, — a large upper and a small lower one. The whole height of this stela is 282 cm.; breadth, 82–85 cm.; thickness, 41 cm. The back face is perfectly smooth. The narrow side faces have two perpendicular rows of glyphs, very well preserved on one side and entirely worn away on the other. The relief on the sculptured

* *Katun* is the shortened form of *Kabtun*, = hand-stone, used as a support for historical and other representations of stucco-work, etc.

side is injured only in a few places; otherwise it is preserved in all its nicer details, but only partially as to its original colors.

On the lower base line stands a man of rank, in profile, looking expectantly up to the god in the niche. He is dressed in a long tunic which reaches to his feet. His head covering seems to terminate in a tiger's head in front, and a plume of feathers falls down at the back. In his right hand he holds a little leather bag tied up with a fine cord, and in his left a flabellum of green feathers with a red handle.

At the feet of this exalted personage is a round altar, the ornamental superstructure of which can only be comprehended by comparing it with the similar representation on the lower part of Stela 11. Here (that is, on Stela 14) also is seen a victim, flung across what is doubtless a tiger-skin and pieces of wood laid crosswise. In this case the face, hanging down over the edge of the stone, is represented in full-front view. Three beads of the necklace are still plainly recognizable. Rising flames seem to meet over the breast, and above them is the bulbous vessel, like the one on Stela 11, with a plume of feathers proceeding from its thick neck. The scroll-work and the structure of beams also recall the decoration on the lower part of Stela 11. Bright-red scroll-work runs up the right and left edges of the niche as far as the curtain, which is divided into four parts (that is, tied up with cords in three places), and has a horizontal band of six simplified glyphs (second manner of writing) above it. Above this band is a fantastic green mask with red eyes and mouth. It is crowned by a diadem of large discs with scroll-work on either side and feathers on top.

All the sculpture described above is in very low relief, but the bright-red god, who sits enthroned cross-legged in the niche, in Asiatic fashion, is in very high relief and is represented in front view. His right hand rests upon his right knee; his left hand, now broken off, held an ornamental pouch with the appendage of conventionalized rattles, which in this case does not hang down over the edge of the niche, but lies upon its floor. The breast is covered by a green cape of scales and a horizontal breastplate, but the latter is very much injured. The bright-red face of the god is smooth and beardless. The lips are wide apart, as if the god were speaking to the people. Large round ornaments are in the ears. The head is crowned with an elaborately executed serpent's head, surmounted by a fantastic little human head. Both are for the most part green, the eyes and mouths only being red. The teeth in the serpent's mouth are saw-shaped. The little head is in its turn surmounted by an oval with the closed hand, which, being contiguous to the curtain, leaves no room for a crowning plume of feathers. Green feathers, however, fall from each side of the head-dress.

Here and there delicately incised glyphs are applied. I can count 4 + 4 + 4 + 4 + 3 + 3 + 4 (?).

Stela 15. Searching the ruins in the right flank of the structure, I found a fragment of a stela, but failed to find the remaining pieces. On this fragment is carved a kind of reptile in high relief. A row of glyphs evidently once ran along each one of the narrow side faces.

Stelæ 16, 17, 18, 19. I thus numbered four large stelæ, the sculptures on which are destroyed.

Close by Stela 18, I found a circular altar two metres in diameter, broken in two pieces. Neither on its upper surface nor on the sides of its cylindrical columns was there a design of any kind. The slab had once stood on three strong columns, one of which I dug up to find out whether it had an inscription or not, but it was perfectly smooth. I call this altar No. 5.

We had accordingly found in Piedras Negras five altars in all: two round ones and three square ones. The Yãxchilan custom of placing round altars in front of all monumental edifices, on both sides of stelæ, and generally in open squares and on terraces, very plainly did not prevail in Piedras Negras. In their stead great sacrificial altars were set up in the principal open spaces common to both the adjacent temples and the deity-stelæ. In addition to these, short columns are found here and there by the side of a stela, probably for the reception of small sacrificial gifts.

I will add here, that the wood-cutters found in this ruined city — who knows where? — one of the little pillars of a small circular table, on the front of which were two perpendicular rows of five well-preserved glyphs each. As the stone — 46 cm. in height, 21 in breadth — was not very heavy, they had carried it to Tenosique and as far down as Cármen, to show it as a curiosity to their friends there. When I returned by way of El Cármen, this long-forgotten stone, which I re-discovered in a hut outside of the town, was presented to me by the heads of the wood-cutting establishment (Plate XI).

Stela 20. Turning a little south of Stela 19 (that is, south of the left wing of the entire structure to which it belongs), a few steps will bring one to a little stela, 83 cm. in breadth, broken in two pieces. The sculptured side, having fallen face upward, is wholly disintegrated; the side lying upon the ground has no sculpture at all. The narrow side faces are also plain.

Stela 21. Pushing forward a few steps further from Stela 20, I found a stone, 115 cm. in height, shaped like the angle of a pointed arch. The sculpture which was once on the front face of this stone is wholly destroyed. The back had no sculpture, but there were faint traces of glyphs on the narrow side faces. In searching for another stone which might supplement the one just found, we came upon numerous shards of incense vessels, dishes and bowls of every kind, as indeed remains of earthen vessels, often of the most delicate workmanship, are generally found in the vicinity of all stelæ.

To the Temple of the Lintel with the Consecration of the Warriors belong no less than ten stelæ: 12, 13, 14, 15, 16, 17, 18, 19, 20, 21, of which only three, 12, 13, 14, could be photographed.

Before we leave this half-pyramid with its temple and terraces, we will turn once more to the two great sacrificial altars 3 and 4, on the ground at its base, which I photographed in 1895.

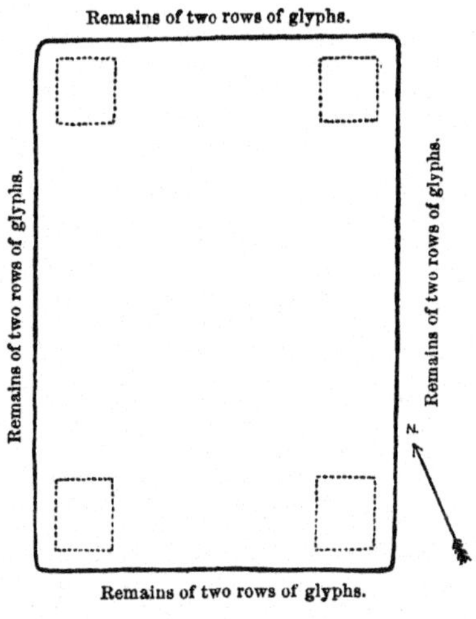

FIG. 23. — ALTAR 3.

Altar 3 (Plate VII, 2, and Fig. 23) is 196 cm. long by 133 cm. broad. The thickness of the slab is 34 cm. It is broken in two pieces lengthwise, but has not fallen to the ground. Around the outside, along the four narrow faces of the table, are the much weather-worn remains of two rows of glyphs. The upper surface has neither ornamentation nor grooves to carry off the blood. The four supporting pillars are quadrangular in section and unornamented.

Altar 4 (Plate IX, and Fig. 24) is 190 cm. long by 180 cm. broad. The thickness of the stone is 40 cm.

This slab is likewise broken in two lengthwise, but has not yet fallen to the ground. The northern face seemed to have traces of glyphs, but I could find nothing at all on the southern face. The eastern and western faces both have remains of a simple design, but not of a glyphic character. The upper surface seems to have had no sculpture, but three grooves to carry off the blood branching out from a central groove are still distinctly visible.

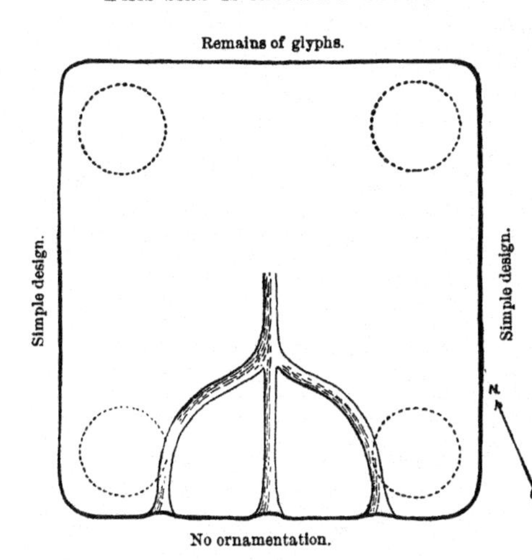

FIG. 24. — ALTAR 4.

Of especial interest are the four death's-heads, 76 cm. in height, which support the sacrificial stone. Their form, however, so strongly approaches that of the serpent's head on the façades of Yucatec edifices, that I am in doubt as to whether they are really to be regarded as death's-heads or as serpent's heads. They all have a small indistinct glyph on the forehead. I think I still detected traces of red about the eyes.

The Temple of the 22d and 23d Stelæ. Going in a southerly direction from the base of the pyramid of the Temple of the Lintel with the Consecration of the Warriors, past the 20th and 21st stelæ, a low rocky hillock is reached, upon the upper platform of which are the scanty remains of the walls of what was once a temple with a façade, that must have fronted north. Upon this upper platform, not in line with the centre of the whole structure, but toward the corner of the right wing, I found Stela 22. It had unfortunately fallen with the sculptured side upward, which was consequently entirely worn away by the action of the elements. The back of the stela was perfectly smooth. The two narrow side faces had double rows of glyphs in a partial state of preservation. This principal portion of the stela, which had been broken in two near the bottom, is 240 cm. in height, to which about one metre more should be added in imagination. The breadth of the stela across the middle is 95 cm.; thickness, 42 cm.

On the level ground in front of the whole structure I found Stela 23, unfortunately quite shattered, weather-worn, and crumbling. It had once had sculpture on both of the broad faces, and two perpendicular rows of glyphs on each of the narrow side faces. The height of the stone must have been about four metres; the breadth across the middle is 105 cm.

With the help of my men I set up the large lower piece of this stela, hoping that the sculptured face which had been turned towards the ground would still be preserved. The sculpture consisted of horizontal rows of glyphs which formed the base of the actual relief. Most of the glyphs had unfortunately scaled off so badly that it was impossible to photograph them. Those that were not destroyed still showed distinct traces of red color.

The Temple of the 24th, 25th, 26th, and 27th Stelæ. Constantly roaming about in search of sculptured stones, we came to the site of a temple with faces west-northwest. A terrace rises on that side only about three metres above the level ground, while at the rear the masses of débris from the ruined temple, mingling with the stones of the equally dilapidated masonry of the substructure, reach far down to the road to Tenosique.

On the edge of the terrace (probably in front of the façade of the ruined temple) formerly stood two stelæ, 25 and 26, which have fallen down to the ground at the foot of the terrace. On the ground, to the right and left of the terrace, stood two other stelæ, 24 and 27. The one on the right wing, or Stela 24, had fallen with the sculptured face turned upward, which was consequently quite worn away by the action of the weather. The back face had no sculpture at all. The breadth of this very much impaired stone is 113 cm. A short piece of a thick column, probably intended for the reception of small sacrificial gifts, stood close by.

Stela 25 (Plate XXII). This stela had fallen from the edge of the terrace with the sculptured face downward, which was consequently very well preserved. The face which had fronted the temple was perfectly smooth. The two side faces seem likewise to have been smooth, for I could not find a trace of glyphs upon them.

The height of the stone — including the smooth piece broken off below — is 290 cm.; of these 190 cm. are occupied by the sculpture, measuring from the bottom line of the relief (not including the incised glyphs) to the upper edge of the stela.

In a niche executed in rather low relief, a richly adorned personage sits cross-legged on a kind of dais, which is ornamented with a peculiar design, meant, no doubt, to suggest a heap of bones. The figure in front view is executed in vigorous, high relief.

From a breast-cape, made of large and small beads, depend three medallions, — one on each shoulder and one in the middle. The god in question holds an ornamented pouch in his right hand. In place of a nose the somewhat impaired countenance seems to have had a depression, to suggest the idea of death, as in the case of certain mortuary images at Chichen-Itza. The two round ear-ornaments are very distinct.

The enormous head-dress is worthy of note. It is formed of a fantastic serpent's head which merges into plumes of feathers on the top and at the sides.

Below the dais of bones (?) is a very irregular ornamental design with a band running perpendicularly through the centre, upon which three footprints are incised. A band of simplified glyphs (second manner of writing), comprising eleven oblong characters in all, runs along the right, left, and upper sides of the niche. Above the upper edge is a conventionalized mask with feathers and scroll-work to the right and left of it.

The stela is finished at the top with two horizontal rows of nine glyphs each, while a perpendicular row of thirteen glyphs runs down each side, making forty-four glyphs of the monumental manner of writing, very well preserved throughout.

Quite at the bottom, on the otherwise smooth surface of the stone, along the bottom line of the ornamented base of the niche, run two horizontal rows of incised glyphs, which have mostly become indistinct, owing to their want of depth, and because the fracture of the stone runs through them.

Only minute remnants of bright-red color can still be seen on the glyphs, the eyes and the ornamentation of the serpent's head. There are no other traces of color left.

Stela 26 (Plate XXIII). When this heavy stone fell from the edge of the terrace, it broke into one large piece, three smaller ones, and innumerable fragments that could no longer be fitted together. The photographs, however, of the larger pieces, whose sculptured sides show no trace of decay, give an adequate idea of the nature of the relief.

The back-face of the stela is without sculpture, but each narrow side face has a row of glyphs, which are almost all destroyed.

I estimated the height of the relief from its base-line to its upper edge to be about 248 cm., to which should be added about one metre more, to allow for the plain part formerly sunk in the masonry of the terrace. Breadth near the centre, 129 cm.; thickness, 30 cm.

The principal figure, represented in front view and executed in quite high relief, holds in his right hand a staff, which I cannot exactly call a lance, because it is curved at the top and ends in an animal's head; on his left arm he carries the rectangular shield, upon the smooth surface of which a design is delicately incised. It can be said of the imposing helmet of the warrior, that it furnishes an example of the way in which the original serpent's head was completely transformed into omega shapes and arabesques. In reference to this question a comparison of the figures photographed by me would, I am sure, prove convincing. The development of the Ω, C, U, ⊥ shapes is fundamentally the same, on this stela, as that displayed on the allied figure of Stela 7, the details only being differently treated.

The surrounding ornamentation of feather scroll-work very gracefully finishes the high omega of the head-dress. I must not forget to add that the omegas almost always, and sometimes the Us, or the ear-discs, are perforated with little holes, presumably for holding little pegs upon which certain ornaments could be hung.

A captive with arms bound kneels on either side of the principal figure. There are three glyphs above one of the captives and four above the other. Here and there on the skin of the personages remains of red can still be distinguished. Other colors have disappeared.

Stela 27. The stela which had stood on the ground to the left of the terrace mentioned above and which I numbered 27, lay unbroken where it had fallen. The upturned face, now entirely worn away by the action of the weather, must formerly have borne the sculpture. I had great hopes of finding an interesting relief on the uninjured face which was buried in the earth; and for this reason I had the stone lifted up a little way by means of the windlass. But, to my sorrow, I found this face to be perfectly plain, nor did the narrow side faces have glyphs of any kind.

The whole height (length) of the stone is 280 cm.; breadth, 110 cm.; thickness, 35 cm. Beside it stood another little column for sacrificial gifts.

The Temple of Stela 28. Proceeding on a line with the temple of the four stelæ (24, 25, 26, 27), we found a little to the rear the retaining wall of a platform about three metres high, upon which lie the ruins of a small temple. Its now demolished façade must have fronted west-northwest, and the edifice could have had but one single apartment. I succeeded in excavating the lintel of the doorway of this apartment, but it was unfortunately quite without sculpture of any kind. On the edge of the terrace, in front of the temple, a gigantic stela had formerly stood, and to this I gave the number 28. It had fallen to the ground at the foot of the terrace, and in so doing had broken into one large and three small pieces. Although the sculpture, executed in very high relief, had fallen face downward, it was so greatly impaired, by scaling off and by the action of the weather, that it could not be photographed. Nor was it possible to discover whether the narrow side faces had once had rows of glyphs or not. The stone must have been about three and a half metres high. Its breadth is 165 cm., and its thickness almost twice that of other stelæ.

The Temple of the Broken Glyph-stela, 29. Ascending the rising ground lying diagonally opposite the last-named temple, we came to the retaining walls of the pyramidal substructure of a little temple which formerly crowned the upper platform, but is now a mere mass of ruins. The temple probably consisted of but one apartment, its façade fronting northwest. Above, on the platform in front of the ruined temple, I found a small stela with glyphs, 29 (Plate XXIV) in my general enumeration, which was broken in one large and three small pieces.

The three small fragments bore the upper half of the inscription in a fairly good state of preservation, and these I dragged down the side of the dilapidated pyramid in order to photograph them in a suitable light at the foot of the substructure. The entire lower half of the inscription, which is on the large fragment, had crumbled away so completely, under the action of the elements, that it could not be photographed. The glyphs were divided into four perpendicular rows of eight characters each. But as the initial glyph occupies the space of two of the others, there are really thirty-one. Of these $1 + 3 + 3 + 4 + 4 = 15$ are preserved.

The stone is 82 cm. in breadth; its height may have been about two metres.

Little remnants of color prove that the whole side bearing the glyphs had once been painted red.

The Temple of the Cleft Stela, 30. On the left wing of the substructure of the temple of the 29th stela just mentioned, and closely adjoining it, rises the much higher pyramidal substructure of a neighboring temple, which is likewise in ruins, and which also fronted northwest. I could find nothing of any importance on the platform among the ruins, but below on the ground in front of the substructure I found a small stela about two metres in height, cleft lengthwise, which had doubtless fallen from above. It had unfortunately fallen with the sculptured face upward, which was entirely destroyed in consequence. To this stone I gave the number 30.

Stela 31 (Plate XXV). On the level ground in front of the two temples, on what might be considered the middle line between the two, but placed considerably forward, I found a gigantic stela, archaic in character, to which I gave the number 31. It was broken into two great pieces: an under one 148 cm. and an upper one 235 cm. in height, and furthermore into two unwieldy blocks, which once filled up the space between the two great pieces, so that the total height of the stone must have been about five metres. The middle width is 152 cm.; thickness, 52 cm. The sculptured side had fallen face downward. The back had probably never been sculptured, and the side faces were so weather-worn that it was impossible to detect even a trace of glyphs. That portion of the sculpture which was on the lower fragment had for its base several horizontal rows of glyphs in very low relief, which have become quite indistinct. Above them are seen the feet of the hero or god. Then comes the fracture, and the sculpture on the blocks which belong between the lower and the upper fragments is wholly obliterated. My men set up the large upper fragment, by means of the windlass, so that I could photograph it. The sculpture is destroyed on the left side of the figure, but what remains proves clearly that it represented a personage attired in a manner similar to those on Stelæ 7 and 26 (Plates XVI, XXIII).

In this instance the hero or god likewise holds in his right hand a crook ending in a grotesque animal's head. The face is framed in ornaments shaped like ⊥, U, Ω, C, as were the faces on the above-named stelæ. Even the little holes in the U and the high Ω are to be seen, intended, no doubt, for the insertion of little wooden pegs, upon which to hang ornaments and trophies. The stela is finished at the top by four horizontal rows of glyphs, which have become indistinct.

In spite of the serious havoc wrought by time and weather, there were still distinct traces of bright-red color visible on the face, the ear-discs, breast-cape, and U-shaped ornament.

The Temple of the Lintel with the Warriors and the Captive (4) *and of the Six Stelæ, 32, 33, 34, 35, 36, 37.* Opposite the two temples just described lies the temple of the lintel with the warriors bringing a captive to their chieftain. The entire structure fronts east-southeast, and the back overlooks the adjacent river (Fig. 25).

Upon the ground in front of the temple, in line with the centre of the whole structure, formerly stood a sacrificial column, which now lies crumbling and half buried in the earth.

From this column a stairway leads up to the first terrace, upon which stood six stelæ, — three on each side of the stairway, — part of which are entire and part lie broken in pieces on the ground. The massive substructure of the temple forms three steps, the masonry work of which is in part well preserved, and is interrupted in the middle of the façade side by a little stairway leading to the upper platform, upon which formerly stood the temple, consisting of a single apartment. Behind, the hill slopes far down towards the river. I was successful in excavating the lintel — 4 (Plate XXXII) in my enumeration — of what had once been the doorway of the temple. It displayed an interesting group of warriors, together with glyphs on the sculptured side, which was lying face downward on the ground and which had been its under side before it fell.

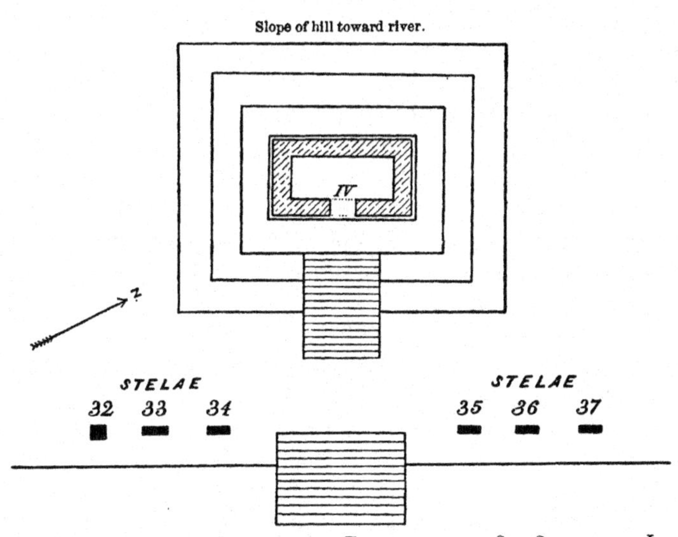

Fig. 25. — Piedras Negras: Plan of the Temple of the Six Stelæ, and Lintel 4.

Length of the stone, corresponding to the lengthwise position of the sculpture, 124 cm.; actual length of sculpture, 109 cm.; breadth of the stone corresponding to the height of the picture (also thickness of wall), 120 cm.; actual height of picture (exclusive of the lowest incised glyphs), 92 cm.; thickness of the stone, 22 cm. and a little more.

Two kneeling warriors, armed with lances, are bringing a captive with bound arms, before the Halachvinic. Behind the prisoner are piled up the spoils of war, among which is an idol (?) standing upside down. The chieftain holds a large lance in his right hand, and with his left arm he presses to his body an object ornamented with feathers. An especially striking feature of this relief is the gigantic globular head-dress, which seems to be meant to represent an animal, since a conventionalized eye can be recognized in the ornamental projection in front. On top of this scale-covered globe rises a plume of feathers. A similar head-dress has been found only on the principal figure of the sculpture on the broken lintel No. 5, belonging to one of the acropolis temples.

Above the group of warriors seven horizontal rows of glyphs are disposed according to the available space. I counted 8 + 8 + 10 + 10 + 15 + 15 + 15, that is, 81 in all, most of which have unfortunately crumbled away, only about one-quarter of them being well preserved. Below, by the side of the Halachvinic, there is another perpendicular row of three glyphs. Below the base line of the sculpture runs a faintly incised row of eleven glyphs, seven of which are still well preserved. Traces of bright-red color were still to be seen on the border, on the arms of the principal figure, and on the glyphs. All other colors had disappeared.

Stela 32 (Plate XXVI, 1). The height of this stone is 251 cm., 205 of which are occupied by sculpture. Lower breadth, 50 cm.; thickness, 48 cm.

This stone, which from its shape might be called an obelisk, has sculptures on three sides; only the back, which was turned skyward in falling, showed no trace of sculpture. The face, which formerly fronted the square, displays a personage of rank with three large glyphs above his head. I photographed this face, being the one best preserved. One of the very slightly narrower side faces also has a personage of rank; the other has two or three perpendicular rows of glyphs, now very indistinct. None of the faces show any trace of color.

Stela 33 (Plate XXVI, 2). The height of this stone is 275 cm., 215 of which are occupied by sculpture. Breadth at the base line, 75 cm., at the top, 88 cm.; thickness, 42 cm.

Upon a throne ornamented with a conventionalized face, scroll-work, and masks of human faces, sits a personage, presumably a divinity, in Asiatic fashion, whose most conspicuous adornments are three great medallions, — one on the breast and one on each shoulder. The elaborated helmet is of considerable size, and has on the front a kind of conventionalized bird with large eyes.

A personage, possibly a priest, clad in a closely clinging garment, stands before the divinity presenting a kind of helmet, *copilli*. A remarkable feature of this relief is a little fish, *michin*, springing from the head-dress of the priest towards the plume of feathers on the *copilli*. The upper end of the stela is so badly crumbled that it must remain doubtful whether it had rows of glyphs or some other ornamentation.

Above the little fish an L-shaped row of six glyphs, together with the edge of the stela and the lower line of the ornamentation at the top, form a square, within which an oblong character is executed in scroll-work, that may possibly have some chronological significance. 2 + 3 little glyphs behind the personage supposed to be a priest have become indistinct.

This entire bas-relief had evidently been most carefully executed and for the most part covered with red polished stucco, but it is now very much impaired. The two narrow side faces have two perpendicular rows of glyphs, which are now almost wholly obliterated. Probably there was no sculpture on the much weather-worn back face of the stela. The divinity of this relief seems to be identical with the one on Stela 12. In some respects this sculpture recalls the well-known oval picture in one of the interior structures of the principal palace at Palenque.

Stela 34 (Plate XXVII). In spite of its very considerable thickness, this stone was broken in two pieces, but the delicately executed sculpture, which had fallen face downward, was very well preserved.

Whole height of the stone is exactly three metres, 218 cm. of which are covered by the sculpture. Breadth at the top, one metre; near the bottom, 79 cm.; thickness, 60 cm.

The back of the stela is smooth. One of the narrow side faces once had five perpendicular rows of glyphs; the other is so weather-worn that it is impossible to say whether it was ornamented with glyphs or with a figure.

The broad face which is sculptured is wholly occupied by a single figure, the great warrior Huech (*hwet*) = armadillo. On the heel protectors of his footwear delicately incised bones can be discerned, as an indication that the brave warrior Huech scatters death wherever he goes. A string of beads fastens a small head below each knee. Above his loin-cloth the figure wears an extremely wide band or girdle, which entirely covers the abdomen. The breast-cape of cylindrical and round beads is ornamented with three handsome face-masks, — one on each shoulder and one in the middle of the breast. A large face mask, attached to a strap around his neck, hangs down in front. The warrior rests his right hand on his hip; on his left arm hangs the shield with a pouch or ornament hanging from the shield. Upon the smooth surface of the square shield is delicately incised the horribly masked, fear-inspiring figure of a warrior. In place of the ear there is a small deep hole, intended, no doubt, to hold the round ear-peg. The head is covered by an armadillo, whose head has a human face notwithstanding the addition of ears peculiar to the animal. The armadillo is surmounted by a certain superstructure, which is very badly impaired; a bunch of feathers on top falls over backward. A few miniature glyphs are incised here and there on the edge of the stela. There are traces of bright red on the arms, thighs, girdle, pouch, knee ornaments, buskins, etc. All other colors have disappeared.

Stela 35 (Plate XXVIII). This was broken in one large and five smaller pieces, but, the sculptured side having fallen face downward, the relief was admirably preserved. Some of the pieces had fallen down to the ground in front of the pyramid. The two largest I was able to set up on the terrace. My picture, fitted together under such difficulties, came out very well indeed in the end.

The total height of the stone is 270 cm, 215 of which are covered by the sculpture. Breadth towards the middle, one metre; thickness, 41 cm.

The back is plain. The narrow side faces have double rows of glyphs, which are now mostly destroyed. The bas-relief of the sculptured face is sunk about 4 cm. below the surface of the stone, though the face of the principal figure in front view is executed wholly in high relief. It is, on the whole, a very admirable piece of work, executed on extra-hard, light-yellow limestone.

The warrior holds in his right hand a lance, on his left arm his shield and pouch. Here also the smooth surface of the shield has a delicately incised design. A little head is fastened under each knee with a string of beads. Above the obliquely crossed loin-cloth is the girdle ornamented with sea-shells. To the breast-cape of cylindrical and round beads are attached certain ornaments with five points. The round ear-discs have each a small, deep hole for the insertion of some additional ornament Above the charming, beardless face an omega diadem forms the base of a great, round head-dress, which is obliquely intersected by an ornament having a glyphic oval in the middle. The broad feathers of the wild turkey (called *pavo del monte* by the Spaniards, *cuts* by the Mayas) mingled with feather scroll-work surround the strange head-dress.

To the right of the warrior crouches a captive with arms bound. Above the latter are four glyphs. Remains of bright-red color are distinctly visible on the warrior's face. The sea-shell border of the girdle, the pouch of the shield, and the background are likewise red. All other colors have disappeared.

Stela 36 (Plate XXIX). Height of this stone is 229 cm.; breadth, 95 cm.; thickness, 35 cm. The back and narrow side faces are plain. The front face has four vertical rows of glyphs with eight little squares to each row; but as the initial glyph occupies the space of two, there are actually but thirty-one in all. As the inscription lay face downward, it is in a satisfactory state of preservation. It was covered, as usual, with a thin coating of stucco, polished and painted bright red, of which traces are still visible.

Stela 37. This stela, the largest of the six, had unfortunately fallen with the sculptured face upward, which was therefore wholly destroyed. The back is plain. One of the narrow side faces has two vertical rows of glyphs, still partly preserved; the other has only one row of larger glyphs.

The stone, now broken into one large and several small pieces, must have been about three metres high. Breadth, 126 cm.; thickness, 50 cm.

After having thoroughly examined the terraces and temple described above, my men and I felt convinced that it would be quite impossible to find more stelæ in Piedras Negras, because we had so carefully explored the entire forest in which the ruins lie, unless, of course, another suburb should be discovered higher up the stream from the sacrificial rock.

We had discovered and examined in all no less than thirty-seven stelæ, of which twenty-three were photographed and fourteen were rejected as no longer fit for that purpose.

As for sculptured lintels, we were of the opinion that excavations among the ruins of certain temples might bring to light a few more, but only a few, since a sculptured lintel is always a rarity.

I would add to my report the information that a large thin lintel — which we will call No. 6 — had been previously found by wood-cutters and taken to the *Casa Principal*, where, laid upon posts, it had served as a table. On what was formerly its under side it had an incised design, consisting of a threefold crossing, which intersects a circle of 30 cm. in diameter, or, to express myself differently, a wheel with six spokes, the ends of which projecting beyond the periphery of the circle are, in a certain way, connected. In 1895 I made a copy of this design (Fig. 26).

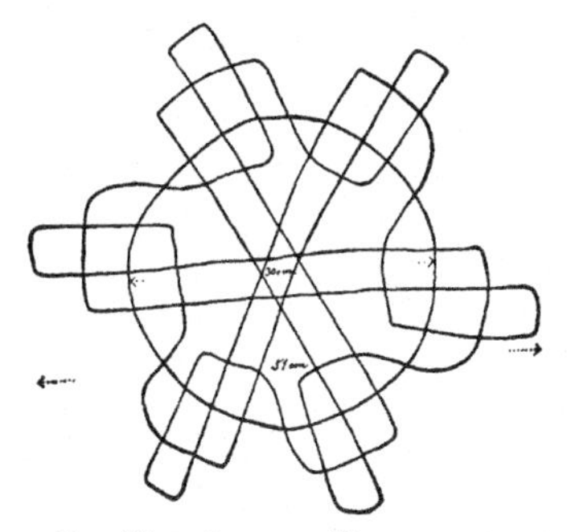

FIG. 26. — INCISED DESIGN UPON LINTEL 6.

I afterwards discovered similar wheels: one on a lintel of one of the five temples belonging to the large five-fold temple at El Cayo; another on the lintel of an edifice built on the southern side of the temple square at La Mar; and still another cut into the smooth horizontal face of the wide rocky shore of San Lorenzo. Lintel No. 6, mentioned above, when found by me, was 134 cm. in length, but it must once have been larger, since it had a piece broken off one end. Breadth, 125 cm.; thickness, 9 cm. When the *Casa Principal* fell in ruins, the lintel was buried under the débris of palmleaves, and is now overgrown by the densest vegetation.

Our life in the wet forests by day and under shelter of the caves by night was full of hardships, and we had repeatedly to contend with dangerous fevers. But our daily bath in the refreshing water of the Usumatsintla, which often rose high above the sacrificial rock, together with ample provisions and now and then a dose of quinine, helped us through. In the beginning of December, 1899, — at the end of the rainy season, — we were able to begin our journey to Yāxchilan, where we were quite as successful as we had been at Piedras Negras.

TEOBERT MALER.

Oversized
Foldout

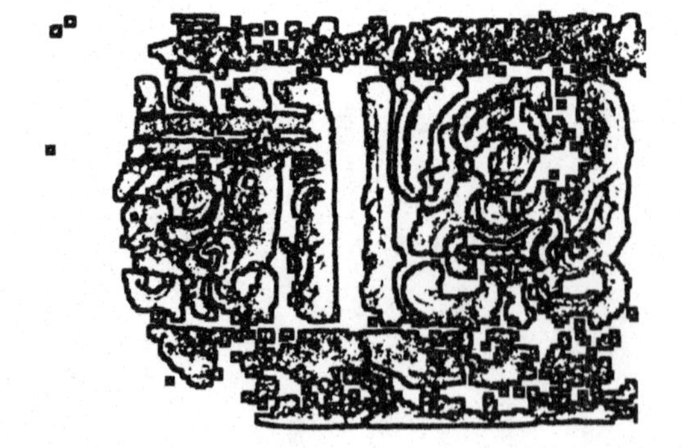

CHINIKIHÁ: SCULPTURED GLYPHS UPON FRONTAL FACES OF

Cháncala: Waterfall, Rio Cháncala.

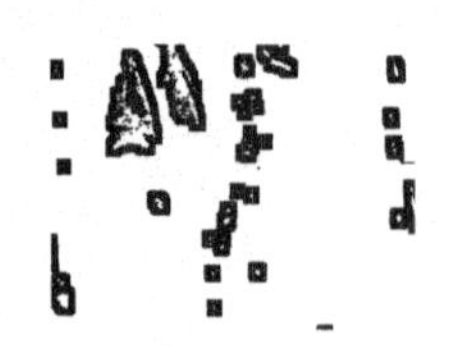

LAKE PETHÁ.

1. Maler's Men and Lacantun Indians in Cayucos.
2-5. Lacantun Indians.
6. Incense Vessels from the "House of the Dead Brother."

CO., BOSTON

NEAR SACRIFICI

2. PIEDRAS NEGRAS: ALTAR 3.

ELIOTYPE CO., BOSTON.

Piedras Negras: Altar 1.

PIEDRAS NEGRAS: ALTAR 4.

Piedras Negras: One of the Supports of Altar 2.

2, Stela 5.

Piedras Negras: Stelæ 2, 5 and 6.

Piedras Negras: Stela ".

1. Stela 9.

2. St

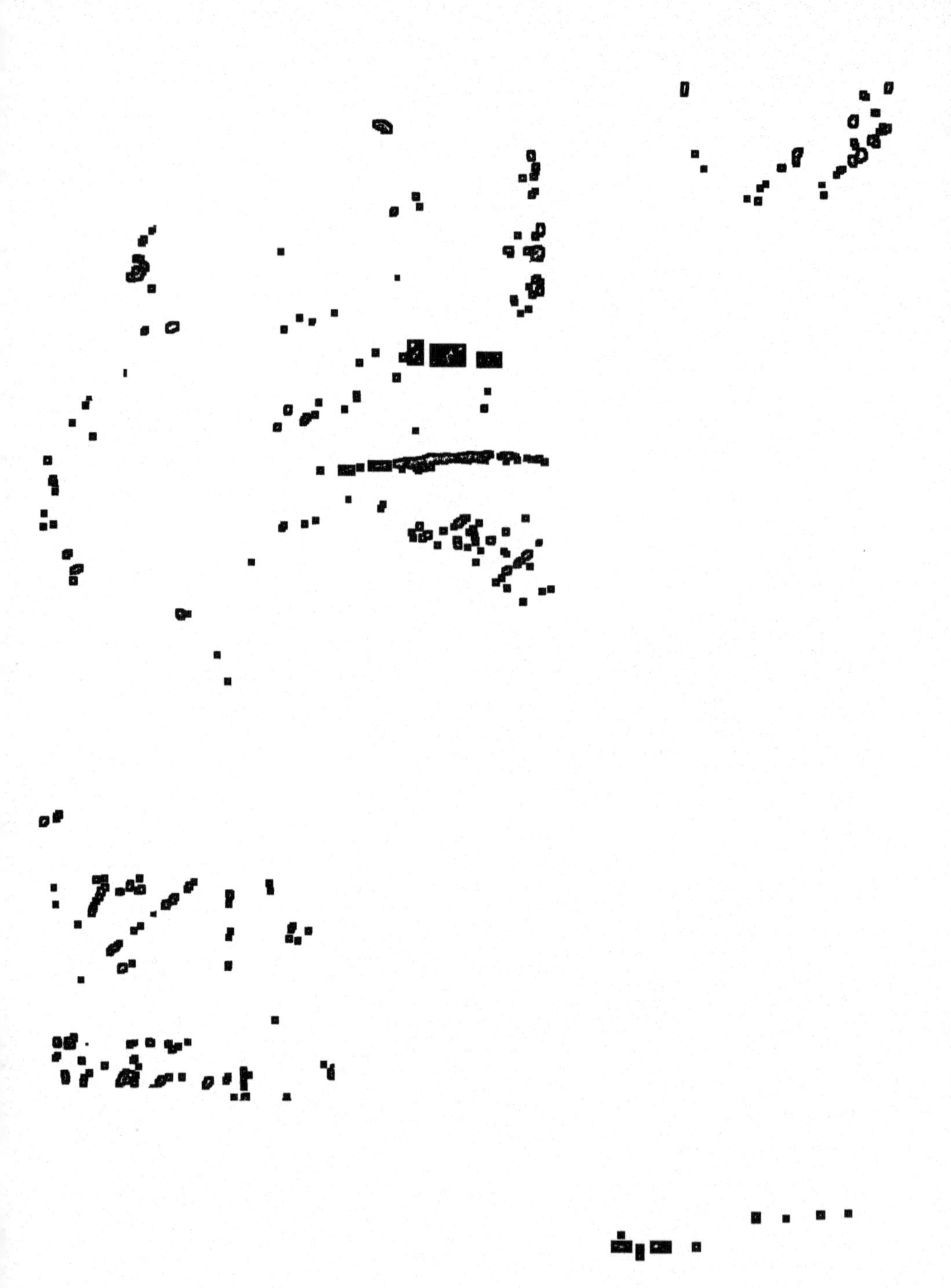

Piedras Negras: Stela 10.

Oversized Foldout

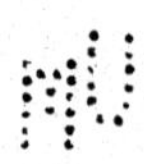

Piedras Negras: Stela 29.

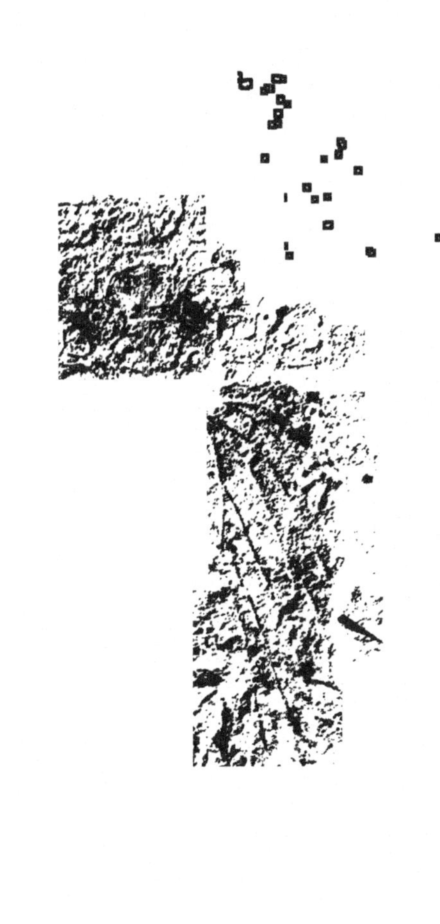

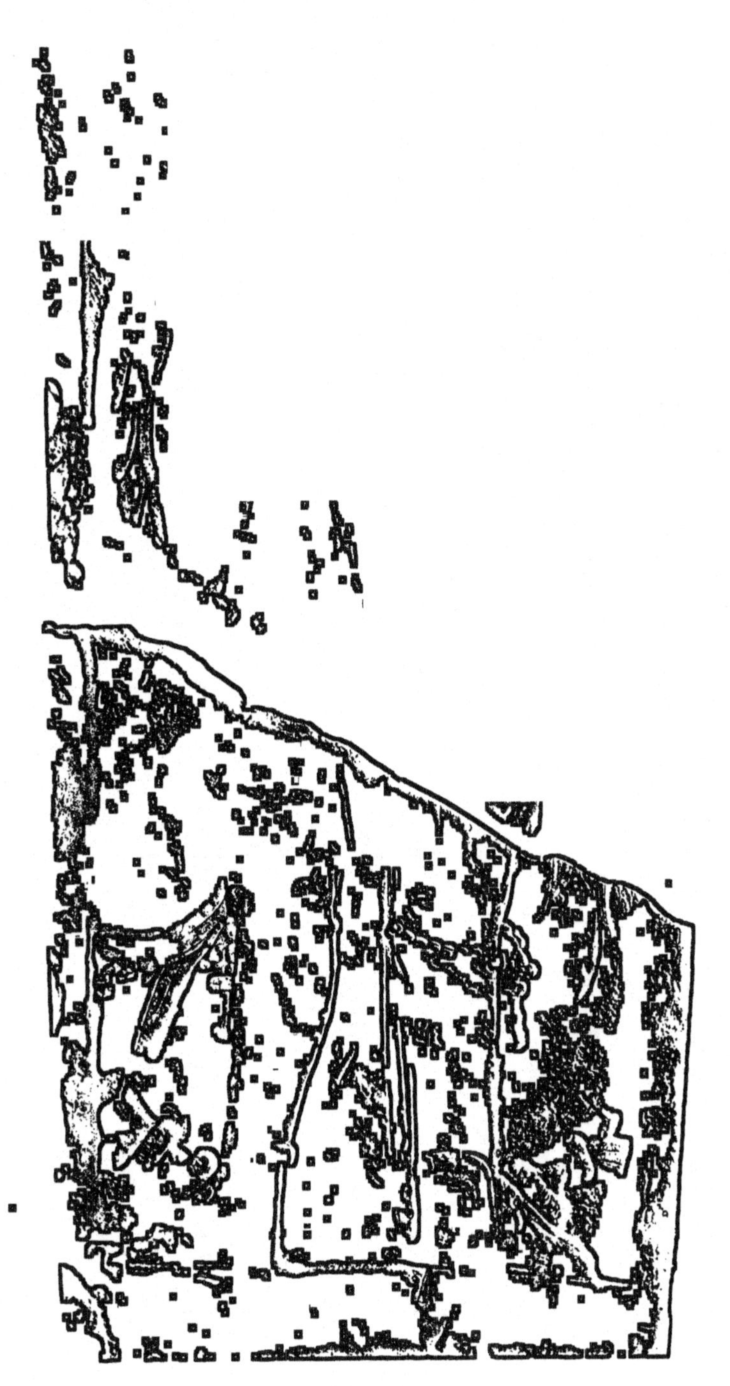

Piedras Negras: Fragment of Lintel 1.